PITTSBURGH THEOLOGICAL MONOGRAPH SERIES

THE TALE OF THE TELL

Archaeological Studies by Paul W. Lapp

Edited by

NANCY L. LAPP

THE PICKWICK PRESS

PITTSBURGH, PENNSYLVANIA

1975

Library of Congress Cataloging in Publication Data

Lapp, Paul W
    The tale of the tell.

    (Pittsburgh theological monograph series ; no. 5)
    Includes bibliographical references and index.
    1. Excavations (Archaeology)--Palestine. 2. Pales-
tine--Antiquities. I. Title. II. Series.
DS108.9.L3   220.9'3   75-5861
ISBN 0-915138-05-0

PREFACE

This year marks a half century of active participation in field archaeology for Pittsburgh Theological Seminary. The publication of this book coincides with the celebration of "Fifty Years of Archaeology" for Pittsburgh Theological Seminary and its parent institutions. It is fitting that studies by Paul W. Lapp should mark the occasion since two of the excavations he directed were in cooperation with Pittsburgh Seminary and the last two years of his life were spent as a member of the faculty as Professor of Old Testament and Archaeology.

It was in 1924 that Dr. M. G. Kyle, President of Xenia Theological Seminary, and Professor W. F. Albright, Director of the American School of Oriental Research in Jerusalem, formed the first joint undertaking of the American Schools and the first field archaeological work of Pittsburgh Theological Seminary. The site chosen was Bâb edh-Dhrâ', a third millenium B.C. settlement on the southeast shore of the Dead Sea. Forty-one years later Paul Lapp returned to excavate the huge cemetery (see Chapter X), and this spring, fifty-one years later, Walter Rast and Thomas Schaub, colleagues and students of Paul's, plan to return to continue excavations in the cemetery and town and to explore the whole area of the southern Ghor where they have located four more towns of the Early Bronze age.

It has been a half century of archaeological activity for Pittsburgh Theological Seminary. In the late 1920's and early 1930's Professor James L. Kelso joined Dr. Kyle and Professor Albright to work at Tell Beit Mirsim and then Bethel. After the Second World War Professor Kelso continued the work at Bethel and also carried on a campaign at New Testament Jericho and Khirbet en-Nitla. In the 1960's the seminary excavated at Ashdod jointly with the Carnegie Museum of Pittsburgh and the Israel Department of Antiquities. Most recently joint Pittsburgh Theological Seminary-American Schools of Oriental Research campaigns were held in 1964 at Tell el-Fûl and 1967 at Tell er-Rumeith with Paul Lapp as archaeological director and Professors James L. Kelso and Howard K. Jamieson as co-directors (see Chapters VIII and XI).

It is a privilege to be a small part of this history. It is hoped that the scholarship of Paul Lapp may be a credit to Pittsburgh Theological Seminary's archaeological studies and an inspiration to future work.

Nancy L. Lapp
Pittsburgh Theological Seminary
December 5, 1974

CONTENTS

PLATES

Photographs by Paul W. Lapp. Plans, Pls. 1 & 29 by R. T. Schaub,
Pl. 2 by G. R. H. Wright, Pls. 4 & 8 by M. J. B. Brett, Pls. 13 &
19 by D. L. Voelter, and Pl. 16 by O. Unwin and J. A. Graham.

INTRODUCTION

Nancy L. Lapp

At the time of his death in April 1970, Paul Lapp had three
chapters completed for an "Archaeology of Palestine". In a semi-
popular way he had hoped to present the contemporary scene of
Palestinian archaeology in terms of the most up-to-date methodology
and the excavations currently in the field, together with a synthesis of their latest contributions to the history of Palestine.
Because we had recently returned from being "on the spot" in
Palestine for over ten years, during which time an extraordinary
amount of archaeological work had been carried on, he felt that
such a book was timely. W. F. Albright's The Archaeology of
Palestine had not been revised since 1960 and had been first
published in 1949, both preceding the recent torrent of excavations.
This was not to be a highly technical work, but one sufficient for
students of archaeology, teachers and professors particularly in
the Biblical fields, and interested laymen.

These first three chapters were introductory, concerned with
such matters as the tasks of an archaeologist, how he prepares for
a dig, and how he goes about it. To conclude the third chapter
Paul intended to present his chronological framework. In succeeding chapters the various periods of Palestinian history would be
presented chronologically with an up-to-date discussion of archaeology's contribution. He had a vast amount of material in hand, as
is evident from the files of notes, articles, and references he had
collected for each period. Some sections had already been developed
in published form, as for example, his article in the Glueck Festschrift, "Palestine in the Early Bronze Age".

The introductory chapters were in mimeographed form, and Paul
had made wide use of them in his archaeology classes at Pittsburgh
Theological Seminary. Since his death, when I have taught archaeology classes and had inquiries concerning the "how" of archaeology,
I have time and again referred to this material. In addition, a
number of colleagues, friends, and students of Paul's have encouraged
me to have them published so they would be available on a larger
scale. I had given thought to this, but there was always the problem
of how to continue from the three introductory chapters. No, I
could not finish the work myself. I would not attempt to write up
the various hypotheses Paul had developed in the past fifteen years.
Although I have a fair knowledge of his work, I had not always been
in on the ground work of his finds and theories. If I would undertake the task I would have to make it my own work, but this would
not result in what he had in mind. Another suggestion was that the
introductory material be published with reprints of various articles

of Paul's, perhaps somewhat gauged to the chronological framework. This was a possibility, but on closer examination it was evident that most of his best works were too scholarly to go with the more popularly written introductory chapters. The work would not "hang together". How to bridge the gap?

Again an opportunity came for publication when Professor Dikran Hadidian of Pittsburgh Theological Seminary mentioned a series he was working on with a local Pittsburgh publisher. At his suggestion I gave more thought to some of Paul's unpublished material. It occurred to me that Paul's own accounts of his excavations could well illustrate the observations and methodology he presented in the three introductory chapters, and that Paul had reported on each of the three digs he directed for a general, non-technical audience in occasional publications and regularly in the unpublished Newsletters of the American Schools of Oriental Research. The form for this book then rapidly came into being.

Chapters I to III define the work of the archaeologist, describe how a dig comes into being, and outline how the Palestinian archaeologist goes about his task. The descriptions are non-technical and introductory; by no means does it substitute for the detailed and thorough training a field archaeologist needs. But an interested student, who wants his appetite whetted, may be attracted to further study. The final section of Chapter III, "Palestine's Chronological Structure," I completed, attempting to take into account the most recent studies as well as Paul's research.

Chapter IV is the reprint of an often quoted article Paul wrote for The Biblical Archaeologist, the semi-popular publication of the American Schools for teachers and laymen. It surveys the archaeological possibilities and accomplishments in Palestine, and although written in 1963, the situation remains much the same in 1975.

Chapters V through XI are selective non-technical reports of seven excavations Paul directed between 1961 and 1968. The reports are chosen not only because of the interest and excitment they arise, but also to illustrate some of the things pointed out in the opening chapters: for example--why a site is chosen, how one goes about setting up an excavation, the logistics of a campaign, the daily chores and delights of the staff, the recording process, and the publication responsibility. They are not intended to present complete or final reports, but they have been edited in an attempt to be consistent with the results of the final campaigns of each site and recent research.

Chapter V describes the ʿArâq el-Emîr excavations, which was the first dig Paul directed after being a staff member of several American, English, and Dutch excavations under some outstanding directors. ʿArâq el-Emîr illustrates the choice of a site in order to further knowledge of a particular period (Persian-Hellenistic) where standing monuments led one to expect results. Hopes were realized in only certain respects, but other discoveries made up for unfulfilled expectations.

At Wâdī ed-Dâliyeh (Chapter VI) work was undertaken to sub-stantiate the find-spot of manuscript finds by the bedouin. The difficulties of the unique type of work demanded by cave clearances and of excavation carried on some distance from civilization are described. Newsletters written shortly after the campaigns cannot help but impart some of the excitment and adventure of that work. Mirzbâneh (Chapter VII) presents tomb excavations as a result of antiquities brought in by villagers during the cave clearances in the Wâdī ed-Dâliyeh. The frustrations and then discoveries are related in the Newsletter. Chapter VIII is the preliminary report of a salvage operation at Tell el-Fûl, undertaken in order to sub-stantiate or refute earlier work of the American School in Jerusalem (which was being criticized by some scholars) before the evidence was obliviated by modern building operations.

The excavations undertaken at Taanach (Chapter IX) were the largest Paul directed in staff, size of site, and financial back-ing. Carefully planned with the benefit of his former experience, the training and preparation of the staff was exemplary. Demands for reports and publication were also put on the staff. The three seasons' work, despite some frustrations and disappointments, was rewarded by the history uncovered, unique finds, and a cooperative and enthusiastic staff. To present this, Chapter IX includes a comprehensive, semi-popular article reprinted in part from The Biblical Archaeologist after the second campaign, together with a summary of the conclusions after the third campaign in 1968.

Most exciting and spectacular have been the finds at Bâb edh-Dhrâ' (Chapter X). Even after three campaigns there Paul was to know only a fraction of the amazing Early Bronze civilization at the southern end of the Dead Sea. The description of the initial campaign from the Newsletter and the summary of the tomb types is by no means final, but should serve to raise one's interests in the excavations still to be pursued. Finally, in Chapter XI, the archaeologist's dream is described, as the stratigraphy at Tell er-Rumeith makes possible historical con-clusions and biblical connections.

The content of Chapters I through XI are Paul's, extracted from the published articles and the Newsletters noted. Only editorial changes have been made, and sometimes footnotes are added to give references or note material available since 1970.

In the first appendix a bibliography of major reports and articles of each of the seven digs is given along with an account-ing of the present state of its final publication. We are in-debted to the American Schools of Oriental Research for the con-tinued interest and the acceptance of responsibility for the publi-cation of these excavation reports, in order that Paul's work may be brought to conclusion. Much has been lost, as the plans and projections of any director live in his mind until they are put down on paper. However, I am much indebted also to the many fine records kept by staff members and the continual help and support many of them give toward final publication. To them this book is dedicated.

Chapter I

TELLS, ARCHAEOLOGISTS, AND ARCHAEOLOGY IN PALESTINE

Archaeology is a love affair between an archaeologist and an
ancient ruin. The ruin heap may be a shipwrecked galleon, an
isolated stone circle in a vast desert, or the fallen walls of a
fortress still uncovered by the sands of time. There are some
5,000 ruin heaps in ancient Palestine, within the modern states of
Jordan and Israel. Only a few hundred have attracted excavation,
mostly small soundings and emergency clearances. Some thirty sites
have been the scene of large-scale excavations, but even at these
much remains to be dug. This leaves some 98% of its major ruins
still untouched by an expedition. Even with all these untapped
resources, Palestine is probably the scene of the most intense
archaeological activity on earth.

Tells

Most of the major ruins are tells. This Arabic word, like its
Turkish counterparts tepe and hüyük, designates a roughly cake-
shaped hill or mound with sloping sides, its layers comprising the
remains of the succeeding peoples who called it home. The Hebrew
of the Bible speaks of a town standing on its tel (Josh. 11:13)
and of making a town a tel forever (Josh. 11:13), that is, destroying it so thoroughly that it would never be inhabited again.
Why build a new town on a ruin heap? Perhaps the most compelling reasons were similar to those which attracted the first
inhabitants to the site. Three of the most important factors were
a convenient and sufficient water supply, access to highways and
trade routes, and a defensible position. While in the flat land
of Mesopotamia tells are commonly built up from ground level, in
Palestine the first occupants usually settled on a flat-topped
rocky outcrop. This higher location provided an overview of the
neighborhood, often for miles around, an advantage in case of
attack (Pl. 15). As its succeeding towns rose and fell the tell
grew higher, its slopes steeper, and its attractiveness as a
defensible site for new occupants increased. Substantial ruins
gave new colonists confidence in the sufficiency of the water
supply and provided their own advantage.
Even after centuries of neglect and abandonment the stumps
of earlier defense walls made renewal of the defenses relatively
simple, and the walls and tumbles of stone buildings provided a
convenient supply for the new builders. When newcomers found lines
of earlier stone walls, they frequently dug them out, leaving their
"robber trenches" to plague the archaeologist. "Robber trenches"

are eloquent testimony to one advantage in settling a new town on
an old ruin. Many newcomers used even more than the building
materials of their predecessors. Often defenses follow the earlier
lines, streets and paths continue a similar pattern, and houses
abandoned for centuries have their walls reerected. It is quite
common to have the same town defense line reused for over 2000
years.

Through the last 10,000 years and down to the present day
colonists in the Near East have settled new sites and reused those
of their predecessors. As a result each tell has its own occupational history. Some have had only one or two periods of occupation,
others as many as two dozen. Some may have been occupied only in
the second millennium B.C., others only for a few centuries in the
first millennium A.D. Gaps in settlement at a site may range from
a few years to a few millennia. Some settlements on a tell suggest
a flourishing town, others stagnation.

Its occupational history is only one facet of a tell's
character. Its setting is another. It may be commanding or vul-
nerable, picturesque or unimpressive. Its location influences
another facet of its character, its degree of sophistication. Its
situation may suggest that it was a cosmopolitan center of commerce
or a caravansary, a governmental center or an agricultural hamlet.
Its dimensions also have a bearing on its character. The depth of
occupational debris varies from a few inches to over 70 feet at
majestic Beth-shan. In extent Palestinian tells range from tiny
citadels 150 feet in diameter to sites of some 25 acres (1/25
sq. mi.).

The small size of Palestinian tells deserves more than passing
attention. Tells can be expanded only with great difficulty. Shechem
in the sixteenth century B.c. provides an example of expansion by the
dumping of a massive fill and incorporating additional space within
the town wall. At contemporary Hazor expansion on a much larger
scale was undertaken. A fortified town of 185 acres (1/4 sq. mi.),
six times larger than the original tell, was created by digging a
ditch to serve as a defensive moat and using the dirt as a platform
on which to erect the defense wall. Hazor is of exceptional size
for Palestine but only begins to compare in size with the larger
towns of Palestine's neighbors. Few of Palestine's towns ever
needed more living space than their tell provided, and excess population could normally be accommodated in caves or hovels near the
base of the mound.

The small tells of Palestine are frequently called cities and
the process of their urbanization is described. To ancients in-
habiting the larger "cities" of Egypt, Mesopotamia, and even Syria,
the fortified sites of Palestine were hardly more than "towns".
Moderns concerned with the urban crisis are likely to misunder-
stand a discussion of the urbanization of Palestine. If "urban"
terminology is retained, accurate communication would appear to

demand explicit divestment of much of its modern meaning and con-
notation. The same applies to "town," but in a somewhat less
radical manner.

Archaeologists

   With this sketch of Palestinian <u>tells</u> in mind, we now turn to
the other partner of an archaeological love affair, the archaeologist. Among archaeologists working in Palestine there is a rich
and healthy diversity, perhaps greater than anywhere else in the
world. Besides local Jordanian and Israeli diggers, archaeologists
come to Palestine from the United States, Canada, Great Britain,
Germany, France, Spain, Italy, Netherlands, Denmark, and even
Australia, Japan, and Venezuela. While directing an excavation is
not a task for the weak, I have worked on digs led by men in their
20's and in their 70's. Archaeology has been pursued as an aristocratic avocation and by travelers indigent when they reached
Palestine. Archaeologists have been attracted to Palestine by
glint of treasure, prospect of adventure, interest in history, and
religious fervor. Archaeological investigation has even been used
as a subterfuge for spying. One excavator is trying to define the
changes in pottery in the 13th and 12th centuries B.C.; another is
searching for the body of Moses; a third hunts treasure mentioned
in the Copper Scroll.
   There are surprisingly few biographies of Palestinian archaeologists, or even brief sketches that convey something of the
personal dimension. Even though scientific excavation in Palestine
began only 80 years ago, the early patriarchs of Palestinian archaeology are being rapidly swallowed by extinction, or, what is worse,
mythologized by tales accenting their eccentricities. The cursory
summaries of the development of Palestinian archaeology usually
present an oversimplified assessment of the contributions of a few
leading archaeologists, and their personal description is frequently
dismissed with a word like brilliant or vain, disciplined or dis-
organized. It seems likely that many Palestinian archaeologists
possessed all these qualities to a degree, but such balanced
assessments have yet to be made of Palestianian archaeologists.
   The four chief expatriate collaborators in Palestinian archaeology, in ascending order of their current field activity, are
German, French, British, and American. Since World War II the work
of the German Evangelical Institute was largely confined to topographical and geographical studies. An active field program was
only beginning to be implemented when the outbreak of hostilities
in June, 1967, forced cessation. Less than a year later the sudden
death of its distinguished director, Martin Noth, cast a further
shadow on the prospects of the Institute. Most of the participants
in annual traveling seminars were <u>Dozenten</u> (university lecturers)

4

in the fields of biblical studies or early church history. Some
of them have made significant research contributions to problems
in Palestinian archaeology, and hopefully in the future some of
them will find it possible to excavate in Palestine.[1]

The Dominican École Biblique is the chief center of French
archaeological enterprise in Palestine. It has produced the first
doyen of Palestinian archaeology, Père L.-H. Vincent. In the last
decade the mantle of elder-statesman was passed on to his successor
and long-time director of the École, Père R. de Vaux (Pl. 7). Both
these men are considered prestigious biblical scholars, but this
has not discouraged them from mastering those aspects of Palestinian
archaeology with no apparent biblical connection. Père de Vaux has
perhaps gained more public recognition than any other Palestinian
archaeologist because of his excavations associated with the Dead
Sea Scrolls, his role as editor-in-chief of their publication, and
his own dramatic flair.[2] After the tragic division of Palestine
in 1948, the Mission Archéologique Française was established to
carry on work in Israel. Jean Perrot, its director, is making
outstanding contributions to Palestinian prehistory. Together with
other French institutes in the Near East, the French institutions
in Palestine are providing unrivalled educational opportunities
to assure a continuing major role for the French in Palestinian
archaeology and related disciplines.

The British gave the first major impetus to Palestinian archaeology with the establishment of the Palestine Exploration Fund in
1865, and they undertook the greatest share of foreign excavation
until quite recently. While much of the early British activity in
Palestine was stirred by biblical interest, its major influence
upon digging in Palestine was otherwise inspired. The British
brought to Palestine the admirable tradition of a disciplined
interest in local history and culture employed in all corners of
the British Empire. This tradition included a systematic and
stratigraphic excavation methodology. The methods are so precisely
defined that the visitor to excavations from England to Africa to
India and beyond can tell at a glance whether the dig has been
British inspired.

In Palestine such excavation has been rather inappropriately
dubbed the "Wheeler--Kenyon" method. Its employment by Kathleen
Kenyon in her excavations at Jericho (1952-58) and Jerusalem
(1960-67) substantially raised standards of excavation in
Palestine to a height not exceeded anywhere in the world. A
number of Kenyon's colleagues and students have employed and
even refined the techniques. Notable among these are Diana
Kirkbride, Peter Parr, Crystal Bennett, Basil Hennessy, and the
Dutch archaeologist H. J. Franken. This tradition has placed less
emphasis on a thorough historical backgrounding, but it has contributed a precision that makes archaeological conclusions much more
reliable for the historian's use.

The contributions of American archaeologists have been more diffuse. Unlike most other nations, the United States government has no Department of Antiquities. This means that the government exercises no control on the character or quality of American archaeologists working abroad. As a result some American excavations in Palestine have been conducted by men without adequate experience or background. Although such excavations inevitably destroy material important for history, both Israel and Jordan have permitted substandard excavation, presumably as a source of revenue and good public relations.

Most reputable American excavators have been associated with the Jerusalem School of the American Schools of Oriental Research. The ASOR has refused to be associated with disreputable excavators and projects, but many excavations associated with it do not approach the standards of the British. Until the last decade much American field work involved joint excavation with the British, but recently there have been a number of larger independent American expeditions at such sites as Ai, Gezer, Heshbon, Shechem, and Taanach. These have been mainly summer expeditions that provide field experience particularly for younger students and professors of biblical studies. With rare exception, Palestinian archaeology is only a secondary vocation for the field archaeologists of these expeditions.

Very few Americans have spent extended periods in Palestine devoted to archaeological work. The two best-known are William F. Albright and Nelson Glueck, both long-term directors of the Jerusalem School before World War II. Albright stressed the importance of understanding Palestinian material from the wider panorama of the Near East and contributed a systematic refinement of the archaeologist's chief tool, ceramic chronology. Nelson Glueck is best known for his widespread topographical studies of Transjordan and the Negev. The eclectic character of American archaeological contributions was further emphasized in the 1960's, while the writer was associated with the American School in Jerusalem. Field work attempted to follow the stratigraphic tradition of the British without abandoning advantages of earlier methods. Emphasis was also placed on extending the ceramic chronology of Albright and upon his concern for broad historical perspectives.

Choosing a Tell

Excavation takes place, we have suggested, when an archaeologist falls in love with a particular ruin. Tells have attractions for archaeologists quite comparable to the enticements leading on a young lover. Tells are old or young; display a degree of beauty, sophistication, and wealth; have a distinctive shape and measurements; a more or less interesting past with greater or lesser capability of

communicating it; varying accessibility; and varying prospects
for the archaeological marriage. The archaeologist's set of
values may differ, though. The British mystery writer Agatha
Christie is reported to have said of her archaeologist husband,
M. E. L. Mallowan, "It's great to be married to an archaeologist.
The older I get, the more he appreciates me."

Of course, there are whirlwind affairs where an excavation
is begun at a particular tell without pre-dig investigation of
the mound's characteristics, serious consideration of alternate
sites, or even careful definition of the expedition's purpose.
Probably the current trend to return to sites of earlier excavation would be less pronounced if consideration were given to the
many untouched mounds with exciting possibilities.

What can be known about a tell before excavation? Does a
mound offer pre-dig indications of exciting possibilities? Most
of the features of tells mentioned above can be described without
excavation--location, relation to trade routes and water supply,
setting, size. Fair estimates of its defense line and depth of
deposit are sometimes possible, but in many instances they can be
deceptive. A careful study of the surface remains, especially
potsherds, will give a picture of the site's occupation history,
though evidence especially for some of the early periods of occupation might be lacking. Further information on the site may
often be gleaned from ancient records, particularly the Bible.
At times aerial photographs, especially those taken in early
spring, reveal architectural features or major installations not
evident on the surface. If a major excavation is in prospect and
the excavator is not satisfied by surface indications, he may
conduct soundings or small test excavations to aid in his decision.

All this information is of importance as an archaeologist
considers what sites are most desirable for accomplishing his
excavation purposes. The Holy Land occasionally attracts diggers
with misguided purposes. A recent excavator's goal was the discovery of Moses' body. His biblical study led him to excavate
at a site where there were no surface potsherds from the time of
Moses. When a visitor convinced him that the room where he was
sketching Moses' bones postdated the age of Moses, he began
blasting the natural bedrock with dynamite, convinced that Moses'
body was further down.

Legitimate excavation goals cover a broad range of interests
and vary from quite general to very specific objectives. My
personal experiences give a fair representation of dig goals.
After the Samaria papyri were purchased, we were guided to the
findspot (Pls. 6-8). The clearance of that spot, deep in a cave,
halfway from Samaria to Jericho, illustrates excavations undertaken to illumine a chance find of importance.[3] During the Wādī
ed-Dâliyeh cave clearance, interesting finds of another age were
discovered in a nearby cave (Pl. 10). At the end of the clearance

a boy took me aside to show me some pots from the same age. When
later we visited the site, we discovered it was the Mirzbâneh
cemetery near the scene of an early field project of the American
School (Pl. 11). The clearance of that cemetery is another illus-
tration of excavation attracted by "chance" finds, but it also
reflects excavation undertaken to amplify earlier excavation results and to fulfill an institutional responsibility for a particular
site.[4]

In another instance, when a group of Old Testament scholars
wanted to form an expedition, they stipulated a large tell,
primarily occupied in the biblical period, and of significance in
biblical history. Because it was one of the few mounds to meet
these qualifications without substantial remains of later occupation, Taanach was selected.[5] At times the historical importance
of a site overrides the disadvantage of digging through many feet
of late debris, as the many excavations in Jerusalem illustrate.

The excavation at Tell er-Rumeith, probably biblical Ramoth-
gilead on the Jordan-Syria border, was undertaken to advance our
knowledge of an area that was archaeologically terra incognita.
A second major purpose was to gain information on a specific archaeological problem, the Iron Age sequence of Syrian pottery.[6]

The excavation at the Bâb edh-Dhrâ' cemetery at the edge of
the Dead Sea Lisan illustrates a dig undertaken to clarify "chance"
finds that had been appearing in Jerusalem antiquities shops for
years and to solve a dispute about the age of some of the pottery
forms not yet recovered by a scientific expedition. Soon after
excavation began, it became clear that the excavation would contribute considerable clarification to our understanding of the
early part of the Early Bronze age, another worthy archaeological
objective.[7]

Perhaps the largest number of digs may be classed as salvage
archaeology. Local departments of antiquities are hardpressed to
investigate antiquities that must be cleared before a house, a pipe-
line, or a highway can be completed. Our campaign at Tell el-Fûl,
where Albright had discovered the Fortress of Saul (Pls. 15, 16),
was a salvage campaign before construction of King Hussein's West
Bank palace was begun. This campaign illustrated another currently
common dig objective, to check and refine the results of earlier
excavations.[8]

Negative factors must also be considered. Our prime objective
in excavating at 'Arâq el-Emîr, west of Amman in eastern Jordan,
was to date ruins of buildings standing above ground, but we would
not have been able to excavate if we had not been able to turn a
path into a vehicle track with minimal expense.[9] One of our
objectives at that site had to be abandoned because of land ownership by a feuding family. The Jordan government would have acted
to secure the land, but we feared a flareup which might have made
work difficult or impossible. Lack of a convenient water or labor

supply can make excavation difficult, expensive, or virtually
impossible. At the Wādī ed-Dāliyeh caves water was donkeyed in
on a six-mile path and Taᶜāmireh tribesmen walked 10 to 22 miles
a day for their work. Such possibilities will disappear as the
sedentarization of the bedouin continues. The weather, too, makes
excavation of certain areas undesirable in winter, and the heat
of the Jordan Valley practically excludes summer excavation in
that area.

Fortunately, none of the expeditions mentioned was required
to have as an objective the securing of artifacts for foreign
museums. Especially British excavations have received support from
museums with the expectation that the contribution would be repaid
with a group of artifacts from the excavation. Practically, this
means that a selection of sites is frequently limited to a mound
where the adjacent cemetery has been located, for most intact artifacts are recovered from tombs, not tells. Other excavations
associated with museums are at times under pressure to pursue
projects with promise of more immediate and spectacular results.
Archaeologists, too, frequently by character or by pressure from
their supporters pursue excavation goals more concerned for the
interest of the public media than for contributions to scientific
and historical understanding.

Such are the reasons archaeologists dig in Palestine--histori-
cal, scientific, circumstantial, practical, personal, political.
Sometimes a single overriding goal leads to a particular mound, but
more often the choice of a tell results from a combination of considerations, and these are revised and amplified as excavation continues.

Biblical Archaeology

The importance of one motivation for excavation in Palestine
is strenuously debated. How much influence has religious, theological, or biblical interest had on Palestinian archaeology? Does
archaeology in Palestine, because it is the Holy Land, have a distinctive branch called biblical archaeology?

Some deplore the fact that Palestinian archaeology is dominated
by archaeologists with biblical or religious concerns to the detriment of the science of archaeology. They point to frequent arbitrary
links between biblical events and archaeological finds, to the bull-
dozing of later occupation to expose the remains of ancient Israel,
and to the popular books claiming that archaeologists have verified
or "proved" the Bible. They criticize especially the current American
tradition for treating Palestinian archaeology as a stepchild of
biblical studies.

Others insist that it is as natural for Palestinian archaeology
to be dominated by biblical scholars as it is for Greek archaeology

to be the concern of students of the classics. While there have
been archaeologists bent on proving the Bible or impulsive in
suggesting biblical connections, they have been more successful
in capturing headlines than in influencing the development of
scientific archaeology in Palestine. Their numbers are insignifi-
cant when compared to religiously concerned archaeologists who have
made responsible scientific contributions. Even those with only a
small portion of their time to devote to archaeology can make contributions to speed the development of the science. As for pre-
occupation with excavating ancient Israel, such concern may better
be attributed to Israel's political and national interests.

Both of these perspectives are largely true, and overemphasis
of either viewpoint would do Palestinian archaeologists an injustice. Overconcern about the religious background and interests
of most Palestinian archaeologists can lead to such wild and pre-
posterous accusations as John Allegro's charge that Père de Vaux
and the religious members of the Dead Sea Scroll team have suppressed
documents scandalizing the origins of Christianity. On the other
side, it is constantly necessary to persevere against an uncritical
use of the archaeological material of Palestine by religious adherents
or popularizers of the "archaeology-proves-the-Bible" line.

What about "biblical archaeology"? It is undoubtedly a more
widespread discipline than "Palestinian archaeology". There are
many more courses in biblical archaeology than Palestinian archaeology available to American students, and books on archaeology and
the Bible are far more numerous than those focused on Palestinian
archaeology. To deny the legitimacy of biblical archaeology as a
subject would be as foolish as trying to proscribe an investigation
into the light archaeology sheds on the epics of Homer. It would
be equally wrongheaded to claim that a mastery of biblical archaeology is sufficient qualification for excavating in Palestine.

At its worst biblical archaeology deals with bits and pieces
of Palestinian archaeology with biblical implications. At its best
it deals with biblical times, concerning itself with all aspects of
Palestinian archaeology in the last two millennia B.C. and the first
century A.D.; and it deals with the biblical world, Palestine's
connections with Mesopotamia, Anatolia, Egypt, Greece, Rome, and
beyond. In such a scope it is as sound to speak of biblical archaeology as it is of Roman or Byzantine archaeology, disciplines dealing with the times and world of the Roman and Byzantine empires.
Yet even so broadly conceived, mastery of biblical archaeology is
less than a sufficient qualification for a Palestinian archaeologist.[10]

Qualifications for a Palestinian Archaeologist

How do you become an archaeologist? Palestinian archaeologists
must answer this question again and again, particularly for young

archaeology enthusiasts. The answer involves considerable
embarrassment, first, because most Palestinian archaeologists did
not ask that question when they were young. While the situation
is improving, the majority of excavators fell into Palestinian
archaeology through the back door. They may have specialized in
related disciplines like biblical studies, Semitic languages, or
ancient history, but very few have concentrated their studies on
the disciplines required of a field archaeologist in Palestine.
Most of the best Palestinian archaeologists are either self-taught
masters or disciples of leading archaeologists who have gained most
of their knowledge in the field. The brightest prospect for the
future of Palestinian archaeology lies with those young enthusiasts
who decide early on a career in Palestinian archaeology, allowing
more time to master the broad and diverse disciplines required of
a qualified archaeologist.

A second embarrassment is that there is no general agreement
upon a satisfactory academic program to prepare qualified Palestinian
excavators. Some would prefer a training program emphasizing methods
of digging, observing, recording, classifying, analyzing, comparing,
and publishing archaeological material. Others feel that academic
preparation should concentrate upon a broader training in the
languages, literatures, histories, and archaeological findings of
Palestine and her Near Eastern neighbors. With this background,
the practical aspects of digging, observing, and such, can be more
effectively learned in the field.

This disagreement is well illustrated in differing views of
what should be included in a final excavation publication. The
first view would insist that the goal is to report as accurately
and completely as possible what the excavator did, what was found,
and its precise content. The publication should avoid interpretations, which should be left to specialists in anthropology, sociology,
biology, geology, theology, the various dimensions of history, and
the like. Those favoring a broader training would hope that the
archaeologist's background and firsthand contact with the material
would put him in the best position to draw historical conclusions
and to critically evaluate the conclusions of other technical
specialists. To this group, those failing to understand their
material historically have not acted as responsible archaeologists.
A recent final report has been criticized for including a chapter
considering what implications the archaeological material had for
the character and origins of the people that produced the material.
While the critic thought that such considerations should be con-
signed to an article in a learned journal, the author of the report
felt his task as an archaeologist would have been unfulfilled, had
such considerations been ignored.

An ideal background for a Palestinian archaeologist would
obviously include the best of both kinds of training—plus development of skills in other areas besides. One important area is

knowledge of the language, customs, and convictions of the people currently living in the part of Palestine in which he works. Just a year ago a new excavation ended in sudden disaster because the excavators were unaware of local custom and tradition. The excavation team left with the suspicion that the villagers were Communist-inspired, and the villagers were convinced that the Americans were cheats and perverts.

The list of subjects to be examined or mastered is all too formidable: study of the methodology of the archaeological process from digging to publication, mastery of the typological development of pottery and other artifacts in Palestine and related material in the Near East and beyond, thorough backgrounding in the history and archaeology of Palestine and its neighbors, a knowledge of a group of Semitic languages and their relations with special attention to palaeography, acquaintance with current language, custom, and culture in Palestine and the Near East. Even with thorough grounding and firsthand acquaintance in all these areas, a person might turn out to be a dismal failure as an excavation director.

Among additional indispensible qualifications are administrative and organizational skills, ability to work effectively with people, discretion in dealing with experts and their findings, and ability to write lucidly. A scholar with a brilliant comprehension of Palestine's history, archaeology, and languages is not necessarily a comparably skilled organizer and administrator. In fact, it would seem a fair judgment to estimate that very few of the brilliant Palestinologists have had the requisite organizational and administrative ability to bring a large excavation to successful fruition. The brilliant mind is likely to be determined to control the minute details of the excavation and its interpretation and get lost in such detail. A common administrative failure is to fail to organize for final publication. So many digs expend all their money and energy in the field, the staff disperses, and little or nothing is done about publication, until perhaps a decade later the excavator, having failed to organize his staff for publication, gets out a disappointing final report.

The path of Palestinian archaeology is littered with digs and diggers who fell by the wayside because of personal contentions and squabbles. A large part of these may be assigned to poor administrative leadership in such matters as accepting on dig staffs persons who cannot adjust to camp life, duplication in assignment of responsibilities, dictatorial manners and procedures, lack of an adequate network of communication. Especially large summer excavations are personal relations powderkegs. Professors and students fly to the Near East one day and the next supervise excavation in the hot sun for eight hours. If they are new supervisors, they have to learn the procedures and methods of digging while they try to get laborers who understand little or no English to employ

these methods. Even the best of preparations leaves some staff
with frayed emotions, and after weeks of bearing the heat of the
day and mosquitoes of the night, personal explosions are bound to
occur under the best of circumstances. At worst, excavations fall
apart and disband. Such conditions require an excavator to be a
skilled leader and cultivator of good human relations.

An excavation leader also must have a perceptive understanding
of the pertinent issues and topics of conversation in a number of
disciplines linked to the proper interpretation of his archaeological results. These include biblical studies, comparative religion,
anthropology, anatomy, art, sculpture, paleobiology, paleobotany,
geology, zoology, geography, ecology, meteorology, ceramics, architecture, and even ballistics, conchology, and the like. He must be
able to interpret the chemical analyses of his finds, radiocarbon
and other datings, petrographic analyses, and descriptions of
weaving. He must be able to consult with his surveyor, architect,
and photographer on improving their results, should these prove substandard. He must have sufficient background to appreciate the
problems of these experts, understand the kinds of things their
efficient operation demand of the excavation, have a feel for their
relative expertise, and be capable of critically evaluating their
findings, though in certain instances this will be beyond his competence.

The above requirements demand an almost impossible versatility,
but the final qualification, ability to write, is perhaps the most
difficult to find in skilled field archaeologists. Successful field
archaeologists must have something of a sense of adventure, enjoy-
ment of the outdoors, exhiliration at the opportunity of rallying
a staff to a challenge, eager anticipation of important finds. Such
a milieu is about as far as possible from the day after day plodding
through records and reports and potsherds in a dusty study trying
to write up excavation results. Archaeologists who rise to both
situations with equal zeal are few and far between, and yet without
the plodding on to publication, the archaeologist becomes guilty
of destroying forever important archaeological and historical
material.

If we are to mention a third embarrassment in discussing how
to become an archaeologist with a young enthusiast, it is lack of
adequate college and university programs for developing the skilled
and well-rounded excavators just described. American undergraduates
looking toward an archaeological career are too often involved in
an anthropology major that is more likely to be inbred than to
display interdisciplinary innovation. Those interested in Greece
may study classics or in the Near East may concentrate on biblical
studies or ancient history, but I know of no undergraduate program
that concerns itself with the broad spectrum of skills that a
future archaeologist should be gaining as an undergraduate, though
some curricula provide enough flexibility for the student to plan
such a program on his own initiative.

Graduate school prospects are no less dismal. I know of no
program anywhere where it is possible to undertake a program providing both the requisite methodological skills for the excavator
and the pertinent historical and linguistic skills required for
adequate interpretation of Palestinian archaeological materials,
to say nothing of contributions to the other skills indispensable
for success as an excavator. In fact, no offerings in the United
States provide comparable training in methodology to what the
Institute of Archaeology of the University of London offers. And
I would predict that in a very few years even that program will be
considered extremely primitive, unless rapid strides are taken.[11]
To get the most desirable background the student will have to plan
his own program and include study at other institutions beyond his
degree program. He might select as the institution for his degree
program either one with the broadest offerings in Near East backgrounds and linguistics or one where he can work with a respected
Palestinian archaeologist, assuring that his training included
adequate field experience.

It should be acknowledged that the qualifications for a
Palestinian archaeologist here described are more ideal than
practical and that lack of desirable programs are undoubtedly
related to the small demand for American archaeologists in the
Near East. What has been said is only to encourage talented young
people to begin planning their educational programs early if they
ever intend to be the broadly trained leaders archaeologists should
be. For persons with such training and ability there will never be
a dearth of available positions.

Defining "Archaeology"

The differing viewpoints described above about the role
biblical scholars should play in Palestinian archaeology and on
the character of an archaeologist's training are fundamentally
disagreements on the definition of archaeology. One side wants
to define archaeology as narrowly as possible as a technical
scientific discipline. It is bent on precise step-by-step definition of archaeological procedures and careful quantified reporting
of results. I doubt that a single Palestinian archaeologist would
oppose more concentrated attention upon improving and standardizing
excavating and reporting procedures. Such improvement is badly
needed.

The disagreement comes when one asks how far methodological
advances can take us. Some expect methodological developments
which will place archaeology among the more exact physical sciences.
The goal is archaeology as a tool discipline with results available
to experts in the less exact sciences. This means the elimination
as far as possible of the archaeologist's personal judgment and of

less quantitative judgments about the people who produced the
archaeological material he digs up.

Others would reply that it is neither possible nor desirable
to make archaeology into an exact science. If dictionaries are
correct in defining archaeology as a study of the life and culture
of ancient peoples, it belongs with the humanistic sciences. There
is no clear prospect that disciplines dealing with man will ever
become exact sciences. Such a prospect leads many to shudder and
wonder if an exact human science is not a contradiction in terms.
The point at which an exact science is reached is the point at
which completion of the dehumanization process occurs.

Archaeology is a little like the discipline of education. The
development of education as a separate field of study has had many
salutary effects upon the better understanding of the teaching and
learning processes and made substantial advances in educational
methodology, but as a field, it has resisted the efforts of some
to make it a technical scientific discipline. It is a human
discipline involving people. It cannot divorce questions of the
best methods of teaching from considerations of what kind of
children we wish to develop. So in archaeology we cannot discuss
improving methods apart from considering the kinds of things we want
to know about ancient peoples. Surely we want to know more than
quantified facts about their material culture.

Dealing with ancient people we are dealing with prehistory
and history. Another way of describing the diverging viewpoints
is to say that one group would describe archaeology as a technical
tool providing facts for the historian to consider. The other
considers archaeology a branch of historical research. History is
the historian's own synthesis of ancient records and archaeological
findings.

At his best the archaeologist must also be a historian. If
he is unaware of the ancient records and current conversation about
the people he is digging, many important observations may be over-
looked or inadequately recorded as he excavates. No one is in a
better position to urge the historical implications of archaeological material than the archaeologist who dug it up. Written reports
can never completely communicate the nuances of what an archaeologist observes on an excavation. Besides, most historians do not
have ample time to delve massive archaeological tomes looking for
important material, and many of them have a disdain for archaeological evidence, nursed mostly by irresponsible past use and lack
of personal acquaintance. Many of the historical implications of
archaeological material will never be made unless they are made by
the excavator himself.

The ferment of these differing viewpoints is a healthy one.
The first group will prevent the second from excessive and un-
disciplined speculation on archaeological findings--something all
too common even today. The second will prevent the first from

turning archaeology into a sterile positivistic science, skeptical that much of anything can be said about ancient man. The first will insist that facts and data are distinguished, the second that these must be subjected to human judgment and interpretation. In the end, both will insist upon the disciplined employment of the scientific method in dealing with archaeological material. All available evidence--literary and archaeological-- is considered and from this the best working hypothesis is developed. With the small and uncontrolled amount of evidence so far available for Palestinian archaeology, hypotheses may be expected to change and develop rather quickly.

This task of constantly updating hypotheses is a scientific task, but it is also an art to be practiced by an archaeologist of broad background. It involves a personal selection, ordering, combining, and interpreting of all the archaeological material in light of the most recent findings. This little book is an attempt at updating the hypotheses of Palestinian archaeology, but remember that the findings come in so fast that what you read is already out of date.[12]

Why read updated hypotheses on Palestinian archaeology? They are a tiny slice of man's past, your past. Without a past there would be no man. And Palestine has been the scene of events as influential as any in history.[13]

Chapter II

THE BEGINNINGS OF AN EXCAVATION

An excavation may be the culmination of a lifetime of planning
or the result of an unprecedented find made a few hours earlier in
the day. Adequate planning must often be foregone in the case of
chance finds and of salvage operations such as the surveys and excavations in Nubia before inundation by the Aswan High Dam. In this
chapter we shall describe desirable steps for a foreign expedition
to take as it prepares to undertake a fairly large-scale excavation
in Jordan or Israel. The steps follow a logical sequence, but they
cannot be employed simply seriatim. For example, financial support
cannot be secured without a convincing plan, but no great effort
will be applied to developing plans without prospect of funds.

Funding

A great diversity characterizes the sources of funds for excavations in Palestine. One of the larger current excavations has
been underwritten by the benevolence fund of an insurance company
while a smaller recent project was funded by the United Steel Workers
of America. More traditional sources are university and seminary
budgets, foundation grants, museum contributions, and institutional
and individual contributions. The foreign archaeological schools
have modest excavation budgets, and the local states provide excavation funds, consumed mostly in emergency or salvage operations.
United States government Counterpart Funds underwrote local costs
of a number of American expeditions in Israel, and United States
Agency for International Development (USAID) funds have been supplied
to the Jordan Department of Antiquities for excavation geared to
enhance touristic interest.

It is difficult to specify the financial requirements of an
excavation. A typical budget for a two-month summer excavation
with a staff of 15 to 25 Americans and 150 laborers was about
$50,000 in Jordan in 1970. The amount varies depending upon such
factors as how many staff receive transportation costs, how much
new technical and camping equipment is required, remoteness of the
site, extent of analyses projected, and character of publication.

In Israel the price has been much higher if local labor is used
because wage scales are several times higher. Also the labor force
is so organized that sporadic requirements like excavations obtain
the least employable. Under these circumstances both Israeli and
foreign expeditions have resorted to volunteer labor forces, consisting of foreign visitors, mostly students, who are willing to
contribute some weeks of their traveling vacations to work on a dig.

With volunteers the budget can be kept more comparable to costs in Jordan.[1]

The foreign archaeological institutes (called "schools" from an older tradition) help cooperating excavations keep costs down with their inventories of dig, camp, and technical equipment as well as vehicles. These institutes can carry on their own excavations at considerably reduced costs. On an annual budget of $5,000, for example, in the 1960's the American School was able to carry on two smaller campaigns of two to four weeks with a staff of 8 or 10 Americans and 75 to 100 laborers. Such smaller expeditions often produce results comparable in importance to finds of large excavations, and the likelihood of a prompt and concise report is greater.

Wise financial planning is essential to a successful excavation. One of the quickest ways to aggravate staff morale is to skimp on funds for food and a reasonably comfortable camp. Another is to have too limited an inventory of the equipment and supplies needed in the field. Any sharp practices in paying laborers will cause discontent, but practices interpreted locally as throwing money away will also lead to complications--and the ill will of other excavators. An excavator must know local prices and practices if he is to retain the goodwill and respect of the community in which he works.

Theoretically, an excavator should have a total figure from which he can assign amounts for preparation, the cost of one or more campaigns, and the expenses of study, analyses, and publication. Practically, most expeditions raise funds for a single campaign, hoping that funds will be forthcoming for the next one. Indeed it is part of the British tradition to dig until funds run out, so arriving staff members never know precisely the last day of digging until late in the campaign. Campaign to campaign funding does have the advantage of more flexibility in developing plans and budget for the next season, and it reduces guesswork in projecting inflation and other economic trends. There are also marked disadvantages. It is more difficult to achieve staff continuity when funding puts the expedition's continuity in doubt, but most important is the fact that it is more difficult to secure funds for research and publication than for actual excavation. If the excavator cannot secure funds for another campaign, it is even more unlikely that he can secure funds to carry out the study and publication of his findings.

Major budget items are international and local travel, camp equipment and provisions, excavating equipment and supplies, recording and preservation forms and materials, architectural and photographic equipment and supplies, staff board and room, wages, reconstruction and analysis of artifacts, preparation of final report, and publication. Local labor and staff receive wages and sometimes also such technicians as the architect and draftsmen. Foreign staff members have received no wages, though especially experienced hands often receive travel costs.

Compared to most other scientific projects these days excavations are relatively inexpensive. In fact, certain foundations have refused to fund archaeological expeditions because their budgets are too small to consider. Nevertheless, most archaeologists feel pressed for funds. This feeling is probably more justified among European excavators and the local departments of antiquities than among Americans, for whom there is such a multiplicity of potential sources. It is also true that persons with a flair for gathering funds at times succeed in heading expeditions though they lack the qualifications of an archaeologist. Ideally an excavator should have a righthand man to relieve him of the burdens of fundraising and dig finances.

Scope and Size

In discussing the reasons for selecting a particular mound in the last chapter a number of an archaeologist's typical objectives have been mentioned. However broad and long or short and precise the excavator's list of objectives, every mound will demand an excavation scope beyond his objectives, interests, and at times even his competence and that of his staff.

Sometimes elements of this broader scope are known in advance. Two recent excavations east of the Jordan River were primarily interested in the biblical period, but at both sites biblical strata were covered by important remains of the Byzantine period. Such conditions demand broadening the scope of the expedition to include competent excavation and recording of the Byzantine ruins. At one site above ground remains of churches and other public buildings indicated that the excavation staff should have included persons with experience in dealing with Byzantine pottery, coins, art, architecture, and epigraphy. At the other there were not comparable surface remains, and it was sufficient to have an experienced ceramicist in the field, assuming arrangements had been previously made for consultants in case of important Byzantine finds.

It is inevitable that an expedition's scope will be expanded by finds that occur during the course of excavation. Even after careful preliminary study and surface survey, at times the remains of the periods of special interest produce ephemeral remains and other ages, not even represented by surface finds, yield more substantial ruins. At 'Arâq el-Emîr, for example, one objective was to excavate stratigraphy of the Early Hellenistic period. In the excavation area we discovered that most traces of that period had been swept away by Late Hellenistic operations, but unexpected remains of an Iron age fort and Chalcolithic times came to light.

Finds requiring outside expertise also occur. The Chalcolithic frescoes from Teleilât el-Ghassûl could hardly have been anticipated, and their preservation is a tribute to the excavators. At Bâb edh-Dhrâ'

badly preserved fragments of a mat under a burial suggested a
multicolored design. If any more such evidence appeared, we were
prepared to call for an expert from the section of UNESCO concerned
with the preservation of ancient monuments. It is impossible for
an archaeological staff to be prepared for all contingencies, but
the plans and budget of an excavation must be flexible enough to
deal adequately with unexpected finds as they occur. If this is
not possible, the best procedure is to lay back the earth that so
kindly preserved the find for centuries and arrange security until
adequate resources are available.

The unpredictable scope is one of a number of factors bearing
on the desirable size of an expedition. While the budget places
an ultimate limit on the size of a dig, the excavator has considerable flexibility in structuring the excavation. He may decide to
have a long campaign with a small staff and labor force or a much
larger staff with a smaller or larger group of workers. He may
decide to spend his entire time in the field digging, or he may
spend much of it studying the site and its environs or the finds
after digging is completed.

The excavator must weigh and balance many factors as he decides
on the size and length of his campaign. He must consider the maximum size of a campaign he can adequately observe in terms of his
objectives plus unpredictable discoveries. Is the character of the
stratigraphy too intricate for the proposed pace of excavation?
How can the largest amount of earth be excavated as economically
as possible? Is the expense for a certain specialist worth the
contribution expected toward excavation objectives? He must take
practical factors into consideration, too. Is it possible to
assemble an adequate staff at the time available for digging?
Are weather and labor conditions conducive to digging at the time
proposed? (In much of Jordan laborers are not available at harvest
time.) Do the plans demand more stamina of the staff than is
reasonable?

The foreign institutes tend to follow somewhat variant
traditions in matters of dig size and length. The British and
French tend to have longer campaigns of three months or more, and
the British tend to have a proportionally larger nonlocal staff.
American digs tend to be about half as long with staffs as large
as the British. As a result the pace of American digs tends to be
faster, for in a longer campaign a slower pace is required to prevent "wearing out". I suspect that the main reason American summer
digs usually last six or seven weeks is because fathers away from
their families promise them a vacation during the remainder of the
summer to compensate for their extended absence. There are undoubtedly other factors, but the different patterns suggest that
tradition may play a larger role than objectives and other scientific
considerations in determining the size and length of a campaign.

The criterion that a dig should not be larger than the archaeologist can adequately observe deserves further comment. Many

factors relate to his judgment of how large a project he can manage: his own and his staff's experience; the extent his time is taken up with administrative problems, labor disputes, staff training; the number of visiting scholars and dignitaries he must guide through the diggings; his familiarity with the periods under excavation. The writer's experience is that it is difficult to manage comfortably with a staff of more than 25 and a labor force of over 200 even with a well-trained and experienced staff. More enjoyable and more precisely recorded are digs about half that size, but other excavators with differing capabilites and procedures will come to somewhat different conclusions.

Those who delimit archaeology as a precise methodology would argue that it is not necessary for a single man to observe all the emerging details of the excavation. Different observers' results and observations may be compiled at the end of the excavation. It has been my observation that no two excavators have achieved such a standardized methodology of excavation or judgment of pottery datings. Megiddo is a good example of what happens when all observations are not filtered through a single mind. Results were especially confusing because contemporary strata from different parts of the mound were assigned different dates. If such correlations are difficult for one archaeologist to decide during an excavation, they will be made less competently by committee decision after the dig, when each participant is prejudiced by his partial experiences.

The safest practice would seem to employ both dimensions of observation: keep the dig within the capacity of a single observer and have individual areas observed and recorded by experienced excavators. Then the chief excavator and his colleagues will be able to provide the most balanced and thoroughgoing interpretive summary of results. When this is turned into a final excavation report, the area excavators can substantially prepare their sections, and the final editing and perspective can be contributed by the chief excavator.[2] Like a history, a final excavation report to be a good one must be something more than a committee product.

The skepticism of this perspective about very large expeditions seems to be borne out in the history of Palestinian archaeology. None of the largest excavations have made correspondingly significant contributions to the progress of Palestinian archaeology. The University of Chicago's Megiddo expedition is a parade example, though it could be argued that factors other than size detracted substantially from its success. While excavations like Masada, which are basically clearance operations, can be undertaken on a grand scale, there is not yet an example to show that a dig beyond the capacity of a single overall observer can be brought to a satisfactory conclusion.

The Local Formalities

Foreign excavators are guests of the state in which they dig. For the Palestinian archaeologist this fact has complicated his work especially since 1948 when, against the wishes of the majority of local inhabitants, Palestine was divided between the states of Jordan and Israel by the United Nations. The enmity between the states has made it impossible for an archaeologist to work or even travel freely between the two states. While both states recognize that archaeologists, with few exceptions, wish to pursue their scientific objectives without reference to current political tensions, it is practically impossible to retain cordial relations and very difficult to maintain working relations with both states. The situation has been even further aggravated by the war of 1967 in which Israel occupied the territory of Jordan west of the Jordan river.

As guests of a foreign state expedition staffs are subject to its laws, particularly its Antiquities Law. The antiquities laws of both Jordan and Israel are based on British Mandate law, but both states have introduced contrasting regulations. To be a proper guest an excavator should naturally be well-versed in this law, but he must also understand current practices and procedures of the local Department of Antiquities constituted to implement the law. In the Near East even more than in Western countries current practice is likely to diverge considerably from the legal provisions.

The chief requirement of foreign excavators is that they obtain an excavation permit. This is the same as what was earlier called obtaining an excavation concession, a terminology still employed in Egypt. The new term is preferable because concession is based on the image that the excavator is given the right to dig up the treasures in a precisely delimited area. Applicants to Jordan and Israel are required to submit sufficient detail on the excavation to permit the Department of Antiquities to assess the prospects of competent excavation and publication. In practice both states have issued permits in cases where the prospects were hardly promising.

There are other causes besides incompetence for denial of an excavation permit. If the site has been previously excavated and it is not evident that the expedition has no further interest in the site, it is in order to obtain approval for new work from the previous excavator. The current Israeli excavations at the Western Wall in Jerusalem provide an exception to this tradition: digging was begun without consulting the leading Palestinian archaeologists who had been working in the same area less than a year before. Permits for foreign excavators to dig sites for which local archaeologists have plans or for which permits have been issued to others will also be denied. The current hostilities have increased the areas in which permits will be denied for military or security reasons.

The antiquities laws stipulate that land containing ancient ruins should belong to the government. There was an unfortunate practice during British Mandate times of allowing occupation or cultivation of antiquities sites which has persisted to the present. Both Jordan and Israel have expropriation procedures, but these are time consuming and usually do not create good will among those affected. In such situations in Jordan it was common to make local arrangements to rent the land for excavation.

Aside from land problems there are a number of formalities at the local level, and practice varies on how these are made between and within the two states. If he is familiar with the language and customs, the excavator may carry on negotiations directly. Otherwise he will rely on assistance from the Department of Antiquities, his national institute, his excavation foreman (if he has one), or a trusted local negotiator. These negotiations include arrangements for laborers, campsite, water, electricity, security, and the like. If the excavator works through an intermediary, it is still desirable for him to be familiar with details of arrangements and to become acquainted with the people involved.

It is just as important for him to keep his guest status in mind at the local level as in dealing with higher government officials. Here, too, he must be aware of local customs and traditions. If his labor force is largely Muslim, villagers resent it if the day off is Sunday instead of Friday. The terminology used for making these arrangements in Palestine comes from English, where complying with government regulations and local arrangements are called "doing the formalities". It does not imply that such are not substantial or that they are not done with genuine sincerity. Foreign excavators in both Jordan and Israel are heavily indebted to both states and many of their citizens for their cordial reception and the facilitation of their work.

Staffing

The world was recently exposed to a scientific project which is largely associated with three men, though landing two men on the moon was the result of indispensible contributions by many members of a very large staff. In popular parlance Jericho is Kenyon's excavation, Masada Yadin's, even though many staff members make contributions as important and indispensible to the excavation as the archaeologist heading the team. A larger dig cannot hope for success without a qualified, dedicated, and cooperative staff. Dig staffs work under such pressures and in such close quarters that weakness in any single staff member will quite likely detract from the overall quality of the excavation.

The excavation staff is usually selected by the dig director, at times in consultation with other key staff members. His list

of prospective staff members is likely to include persons both
known and unknown to him who have written about joining his
expedition. Some of these may be students for which dig experience
would be a desirable part of their educational training, and he
may have background on these students from his colleagues. He has
sent inquiries about the interest and availability of others,
especially those with special skills required for the excavation.
Some prospects would need a stipend or could only come if transportation costs were covered; others would be willing to pay their
travel costs and some would even be willing to make a contribution
to the dig budget.[3]

Frequently staff applicants far outnumber available positions.[4]
In this case the excavator's concern is to get the best prospect
for each position as well as the best possible excavation team.
To do so he may apply both general criteria of selection as well
as criteria for specific skills. Among general criteria he might
want to give preference to those with positions or studies center-
ing on Palestinian archaeology or related disciplines, to keep a
balance between new and experienced staff, to secure staff with a
broad range of backgrounds potentially useful to the dig, or to
attract staff capable of writing and contributing to dig publication.
Sex and age are at times important. At times there are advantages
to a one-sex team. Some campaigns are so strenuous that staff
should be limited to the young and vigorous. There might also be
a good very young applicant rejected for fear he may not be happy
without a team peer.

The Palestinian excavator is never in a position to include
within his staff all the skills and know-how that might prove useful.
Essential are the skills of an architect, surveyor, draftsman,
photographer, artist-registrar, pottery chronologist (unless remains
predate 5000 B.C.), and artifact conservator. If tombs are to be
dug, the services of an anthropologist should be available. Of
course, more than one of these skills may be contributed by a
single staff member, and some are frequently provided by the archaeologist himself. In addition to proficiency in these skills it is
desirable that these technicians have excavation experience as
assistants or specialized training before working alone. For
example, an excellent photographer will not do a completely
satisfactory dig job without additional training and experience.
The architect will be much better qualified if he is grounded in
the history of architecture in the Mediterranean basin and the Near
East.

Dig staffs are divided between those contributing the special
skills just enumerated and those who supervise, observe, and record
the excavating. With the partial exception of the British, these
field archaeologists are drawn largely from the ranks of students
and scholars with biblical interests, particularly Old Testament.
This syndrome has had the effect of limiting the broad spectrum of

skills that could be represented in the staff. It is not unfair
to ask why excavations coming from major universities have brought
staffs overburdened with biblical specialists when it would not be
difficult to secure persons with skills in such areas as art,
history, geology, hydrology, meteorology, palaeobotany, data
processing, soil analysis and the like. It is even rare to have
staff competent in Egyptology, Assyriology, Anatolian or classical
studies, even though most large excavations unearth evidence on
trade and political relations with these areas.[5]

Excavation staffs vary widely in quality, composition, and
relative size. On a recent occasion two American School-related
excavations each had some six foreign staff members in the field
at the same time. One employed some 60 laborers, the other 150,
though both had comparably complex stratigraphy. The latter also
failed to have a qualified architect. It is not difficult to
conclude which excavation's results were more carefully dug,
observed, recorded, and reported. My own experience suggests that
in complicated stratigraphy it is impossible even for an experienced
field archaeologist to observe and record the digging of more than
two or three teams of five or six laborers.

The number of specialists for the staff also deserves attention.
The concern for adequate field supervision has at times slighted a
dig's need for adequate staff to process, treat, and analyze the
artifacts and pottery. In most digs the finds could be much further
along toward publication before leaving the field than they are.
In fact, it should be a challenge to future archaeologists to
attempt to push study, analysis, and write-up in the field to the
point where final publication could be effected in a few months,
rather than a few years or decades as is presently more common.

Even if an applicant meets the general qualifications and has
desirable skills, it may be obvious that he should be rejected for
personal reasons. Good morale is essential to superior performance
in the field. Any applicant who shows even slight promise of de-
tracting from staff morale should probably be rejected. This may
be because he would have difficulty adjusting to the flies, smells,
and dirt of camp life, because he has a history of instability
under stress, because of health problems, or because his personality is not compatible with team effort. Some staff members prove
disappointing merely because they cannot adjust to the period of
absence from family or girl friend. On the other hand, I know of
a staff member who did an outstanding job before flying home to get
married the next day.

It seems unnecessary to add that the staff should be selected
as far in advance as possible. Many find it impossible to schedule
two months for an excavation without at least a year's notice. At
that time each staff member should be informed in as much detail
as possible about the excavation, preparations required of him,
his precise responsibilities during the dig, any subsequent

responsibilities, and financial arrangements. If a series of campaigns are planned, it should also be made clear under what conditions a staff member is eligible or responsible for subsequent participation. Clear instructions, plans, and responsibilities are equally essential for effective work and good morale. It is also wise to keep a list of alternate staff, for there are bound to be emergencies which cause staff cancellations.

A final word may be in order about the line of authority and the role of the excavation director. There is no reason why any number of administrative arrangements might not effectively serve an excavation. There are also types of arrangements that often lead to difficulty. There is the situation in which an excavator accepts substantial financial support in return for a substantial voice in the administration of the excavation. If the source or sources have little understanding of archaeology and digging, this is a dangerous situation, for the excavator makes it possible for decisions to be made which would adversely affect the quality of the excavation. The same applies to an arrangement where there are archaeological and administrative directors. It is better if the excavator retains final administrative say even if he turns most administrative work over to a trusted coworker--certainly a desirable practice.

Planning the Digging

Two big decisions for the archaeologist are where and in how many places to excavate on the mound and in its environs. The questions should certainly be answered in terms of the dig's objectives, but decisions will also involve basic differences in excavation methodology. If an objective is an understanding of the tell's defenses, an area on the slope must be dug. Since the objective would be furthered if a gateway could be encountered, the excavator may look for surface indications of a gate, examine aerial photographs, or deduce a likely spot for a gateway from the mound's contours, water source, or the like.

This procedure can multiply excavation areas on and around the mound. He might want to excavate to bedrock from the highest spot on the mound to obtain the most complete stratigraphic sequence, to explore a curious depression with hopes of finding a water shaft, to investigate some massive protruding boulders aiming at uncovering a public building, to dig for cultic material where a chance cultic find was discovered, or to clear areas at the base of the mound in a tomb search. The result is an excavation with a number of areas or trenches, none of which expose a very large area of the town plan.

This pattern is well illustrated by Kathleen Kenyon's excavation at Jericho, where work was carried on in three trenches

and "sites" on the mound and in the cemetery labeled from A to P.
Long before Dr. Kenyon began working at Jericho, W. F. Albright
had observed, "It is vastly preferable to excavate areas instead
of trenches."6 Of the Jericho dig it has been observed that it
is regretable that such a large expedition did not secure the
complete plan of a single pre-pottery Neolithic house because
of its trenching procedures. This suggests that the excavator
should consider a methodological alternative to multiplication of
excavation sites to accomplish his objectives. This means an
attempt to accomplish his objectives by excavation in a single
or a very few larger areas. This last procedure is nicely illustrated by the excavations of Père R. de Vaux at Tell el-Fâr'ah
(north), biblical Tirzah.

There are other advantages to digging larger areas besides
uncovering larger and more comprehensible plans. Relationships
can be clarified, such as those between the defenses and the
constructions inside or between a temple and its surroundings.
It is difficult to document a case for town planning in a confined trench area. Difficult stratigraphy is easier to follow
in a larger continuous area than in smaller separate trenches.
It has often been emphasized that an excavation should leave intact
as much of the mound as is not essential to his purposes so that
future investigators with improved techniques will be able to
correct and refine current conclusions. Digging a few areas will
leave the mound less chopped up for the future. The trench must
frequently be contracted as excavation gets deeper. The larger
area avoids the common necessity of widening a trench to reach or
expose a sufficient area of the lowest occupations.

There is the disadvantage that a single area may not give the
complete occupational history of the mound. Several occupations
and at times all earlier occupations may be swept away by major
building operations. This is why there is some advantage to digging
more than a single area.

If one of his objectives is to get an overall picture of the
occupation of his mound, the archaeologist will need to know the
depth of the debris, character of the stratigraphy, expedition
size, and number of campaigns before he can decide precisely how
large his excavation area(s) should be. The study of the Megiddo
expedition is true of a surprising number of digs. The upper
layers of the mound were the subject of great effort and expendi-
ture, but the earlier occupation received scant attention. To open
too small an area is just as unfortunate. The additional strips
opened can have their elements added to the plan, but photographs
will be limited to the separate pieces of each stratum excavated.

If there is no other means of roughly gauging the depth and
character of the debris, a preliminary sounding should be undertaken to secure these facts before the overall expedition plan is
finalized (Pl. 28). The number of campaigns also deserves careful

consideration. There are cases where an expedition plans to accomplish its objectives in three campaigns and fails to reach them after seven, or where, after twelve years of digging there is no immediate prospect of the appearance of the first volume of its final report. Obviously a final report suffers if it is composed so long after excavation, and the inevitable discontinuities in staff complicate the problem. While perhaps arbitrary, it would seem wise to limit a series of campaigns to not more than five years with definite objectives to be accomplished within the specified number of campaigns. Subsequent publication would not then be too delayed, and a fresh series would benefit from insights gained in publication research. This might seem too long to wait for final publication. It is a compromise solution, for quick publication after one or two campaigns is likely to produce so many typologies, conclusions, and interpretations that require subsequent revision that the result is confusing.

Digging Method

The contrasting emphasis on trenches or larger areas is echoed in the methods of digging employed by Palestinian archaeologists. The area plan of digging tends to be associated with digging methods introduced to Palestine by G. A. Reisner's excavations at Samaria of 1908-10 and employed in subsequent excavations with which Clarence Fisher was associated. It is this "Reisner-Fisher" method which was adopted and developed by such eminent archaeologists as W. F. Albright and R. de Vaux and is still employed by most Israeli archaeologists. Its focus is upon the stratum plan. All contemporary architectual features with their rebuilds are recorded on the plan. Each area circumscribed by walls is given a locus number. Artifacts are recorded by locus and in relation to the floors or occupation surfaces of the stratum of occupation. When excavation of a stratum is completed, it is removed, and the process is repeated.

The trenching method has been associated with the introduction of British excavation techniques in Palestine especially with Kathleen Kenyon's work at Jericho beginning in 1952. In this so-called Wheeler-Kenyon method the section takes precedent over the stratum plan. The definition of a locus shifts from a unit of the plan to a unit of the section. Emphasis is placed on isolating each layer of soil as it was deposited and each disturbance of that layer. Ideally digging involves removing each layer or disturbance in reverse order of their deposition. Each three-dimensional element excavated receives a locus number. This applies to all layers be they silt deposits, fills, floors, occupation or destruction debris, tramped campsite surfaces; it includes each disturbance such as pits, silos, foundation or robber

28

trenches, razings, cistern shafts, erosion gulleys, earthquake
faults, sewers, or tombs; it also means all installations such
as walls, streets, ovens, kilns, industrial installations, fallen
roofs, and the like.

Because the nature and character of layers changes radically
from place to place on the mound, this trenching method requires
that sections be examined and recorded at frequent intervals. This
is usually accomplished by plotting on the mound a grid of six-
meter squares (Pl. 29). Digging then takes place in five-meter
squares separated by one-meter catwalks called balks. Care is
taken to cut the four sides of the square vertically so that the
layers in the balks may be observed and drawn to scale for a comprehensive sectional record. As the final steps the excavation of
a stratum the balks are removed, overall photographs taken, and
plans completed before simultaneous removal of the stratum and re-
establishment of the catwalks for repetition of the process (Pl. 30).

The last sentence deserves further comment, for especially
American digs attempting to emulate British methods often fail to
follow the final steps. At worst digging in the squares is not
kept in phase. This means that digging in each square or small
group of squares proceeds at its own pace so that two or more
strata are being concurrently excavated. The catwalks become
boundaries of tiny individual excavations. Even if the excavation
is kept in phase, the advantages of the British method are lost if
the balks are not regularly removed. The Reisner-Fisher method had
the advantage of tracing a layer of occupation over a larger area.
Such tracing is interrupted by the balks unless they are systemati-
cally removed after their information has been recorded. Unless
the British methods are thoroughly understood and employed, they
may deter rather than aid stratigraphic excavation.

The crux of excavation by either method is the dirt. To the
uninitiated a tell is a heap of dirt and stones. A little dig
experience trains the eye to distinguish hard, flecked layers of
fill from soft gray layers of occupation debris and to note the
lines of foundation trenches cut through earlier floors. But
even highly experienced foreign dig supervisors will probably have
difficulty separating the line of a mudbrick wall from the mudbrick wash against it. It is the experienced local diggers,
feeling the different hardness of the two, who can make this
separation. It is the experienced local technical men, as they
are called, whose year-in-year-out experience makes it possible to
separate the layers and detect the disturbances--distinctions that
go unobserved to the less practiced.

The crucial importance of observing each three-dimensional
element of the dirt and debris of a mound becomes evident when the
result of missing even one of the omnipresent pits in Palestinian
tells is considered. Suppose a householder decided to dig a site
for grain storage in the corner of one of his rooms. He digs down

through three earlier strata of occupation representing occupation
of four centuries. He puts pottery jars of grain in the silo and
as time passes debris, including sherds of accidentally broken jars,
collects in the bottom of the pit. After an enemy burns the town,
the debris is used to fill in the silo. Then comes the excavator
who digs the four strata without noticing the silo. He finds
potsherds of approximately the same latest date in all four strata
and concludes that all four strata were constructed within a
relatively short period of time. If, for example, the period
involved was 1400-1000 B.C., he might attribute all the strata to
the beginning of the Israelite United Monarchy, when, in fact, the
three earlier strata belonged respectively to a Philistine, an
early Israelite, and a Canaanite occupation. So failure to deal
properly with the dirt distorts history--no matter how painstakingly
and scientifically the finds are treated after excavation.

If we may overgeneralize on the employment of digging method
in Palestine, Israeli archaeologists largely follow the Reisner-
Fisher methods as they were employed between World Wars I and II
while Jordanian excavators employ the newer British methods. The
French basically follow the earlier methods but incorporate
salutary British features. Some American excavations have
attempted to employ British methods with greater or lesser success.
Others have tried to combine the emphases of the both methods,
stressing the importance of daily plans of the squares as well as
drawings of the balks, and attempting to use the British methods
of recording in excavations of larger areas rather than trenches.

Staff Orientation

On a recent visit to an excavation, I asked one of the supervisors the relation of his squares to the previous excavations of
Macalister. He replied, "Who was Macalister?" This is an indication
that at least some expeditions slight staff orientation. It is a
common practice for new staff to reach Palestine one day and find
themselves digging the next. Much excavation is done poorly because
of inadequate orientation to excavation methodology and still more
is done without enthusiasm because the supervisor is not aware of
the background, purposes, and broader significance of his particular
finds.

Orientation in this last category is essential not merely for
staff morale. Without such orientation it is obvious that the
supervisor would make his observations less precisely and perhaps
fail to notice important phenomena. While such background can be
supplied in written form or conveyed in lectures early in the dig,
a few days of orientation sessions before excavation is perhaps
the most desirable procedure. It also helps staff orient to time
change and local conditions. Such orientation should also include

careful attention to procedures of digging and recording and a
basic consideration of excavation methodology.

Related is the question of the extent to which an expedition
should be a training operation. Many excavations in Palestine are
staffed largely by persons who want a one-time experience on a dig
as well as others who want archaeology to be part of their careers.
In some instances it would be fair to criticize that the concern
for training as many as possible has detracted from the quality of
the excavation. Obviously, when the quality of the excavation is
lowered, the educational experience is correspondingly marred. It
would seem desirable to follow the principle that orientation and
training should be undertaken insofar as they are compatible with
the highest standards of excavation and publication. Perhaps the
best example of an excavation geared to training without sacrificing
excavation standards has been the Hebrew Union College Biblical and
Archaeological School's excavation at Gezer under the direction of
William Dever and a competent staff. The digging manual of the
Gezer expedition,[7] and similar guides for other digs, indicates the
sound and solid concern for improving methodology that characterizes
present day excavation in Palestine. Undoubtedly our methods will
soon be considered primitive--especially in the area of technical
and scientific analyses and synthesis. Nevertheless, Palestinian
archaeology has come a long way in a very short time, as we shall
see in the next chapter.

Chapter III

DATING THE DISCOVERIES

Contacts with history in high school or college have left most of us with something of a distaste for chronology. At least those in the over-thirty generation can hardly have escaped history courses where the instructor felt that the most that was possible in the limited time available was to emphasize the chronological structure and key events and persons of the period, and the study of history boiled down to memorizing a chronological framework, the dates of kings, and dynastic charts. Does it really matter whether Columbus discovered America in 1392, 1492, or 1592?

Chronology and history

In a general sense precise chronology is not essential to historical appreciation and understanding. For one lacking a clear perception of the course of events of the 14th, 15th, and 16th centuries, misdating the discovery of America by a century hardly distracts from whatever significance the event has for him. It would be unrealistic to argue that if a person thought the event took place in 1392, his knowledge of the event would cease to have meaning or importance, or even that remembering 1492 adds to the significance of this historical event for him. Such a perspective tends to confirm a prejudice against overemphasis on chronology in the study of history.

On the other hand, consider the havoc if a historian were to take such a cavalier attitude toward chronology. He might easily conclude that the discovery of America was the result of the creative forces unleashed by the Reformation or an attempt to test the theory of Copernicus. It is important for the historian to reckon with the fact that Copernicus was nineteen when America was discovered. A historian can do little with persons or events which cannot be fitted into a rather precise chronological framework.

It follows that if archaeological material is to be of historical value, it must be as precisely dated as possible. For example, an archaeologist discovers a major destruction of a Palestinian town and concludes that the evidence points to a date between 1250 and 1150 B.C. Without further evidence or a more precise dating, it would be impossible to decide whether the destruction was the result of internecine warfare between Canaanite towns, an Egyptian campaign, Israelite tribal conquest, or an attack by a Sea People. Is archaeology able to provide datings precise enough to be of historical value?

Scholars disagree on an answer to this question. Sober replies would vary from sometimes to almost never. One competent scholar

concludes that the evidence points to an identification of certain
ruins with Saul's fortress as the best hypothesis. Another insists
that the evidence is too meager to justify such a postulation. Such
positions tend to become overpolarized when the weaknesses and
tentativeness of the best hypothesis are not emphasized or when the
"best" hypothesis is ignored as one among several interpretive
options. What is a desirable modus operandi? It seems clear that
when the "best" hypothesis seems improbable or unconvincing, it
might well be dismissed and the material left a conundrum. In
other cases it seems desirable to define the best interpretation
of the evidence, even if it is necessary to stress the speculative
nature of the postulation.

Working hypotheses, refined as new evidence appears, are a
requirement of the scientific method and have proved more productive
in archaeology than more skepticial approaches. This can be noted
by even casual excavation visitors. It is quite common to be conducted through an excavation where descriptions range from: "This
is either Late Hellenistic or Early Roman"; to "We won't know
exactly what this is until we've studied the material after the
excavation"; to "We haven't figured this out yet; can you help us?"
More often than not the hoped for advances in interpretation fail
to materialize after excavation. In any event, post-dig interpretations lose the benefit of having been refined in the field as the
stream of relevant evidence was emerging.

From this perspective I tend to feel that archaeological
material is sometimes susceptible of sufficient chronological
precision to be of historical importance. After all, the evidence
of ancient history is so limited that very few statements approach
the indubitable. To illustrate, Ahab was killed in a battle near
Ramoth-gilead about 850 B.C. The probable site of Ramoth-gilead
suffered a major destruction about the middle of the ninth century
B.C. The identification of the site is not indubitable. The
destruction could have occurred a few years before Ahab's death
when a cow kicked over a lamp or a few years thereafter when an
enemy set his neighbor's grain heap ablaze. Yet, the best hypothesis
based on the extant evidence would connect the destruction with the
battle in which Ahab was killed.

Where is the line to be drawn between such hypotheses and the
objectionable practice of overcorrelation of biblical and archaeological material? It takes well-balanced judgment to draw that
line appropriately, and no two historians would draw it at exactly
the same point. It may be observed that advances in archaeological
precision make connections more and more viable. It is now
frequently possible to date archaeological groups within a quarter-
or half-century. Correlations with such material are certainly
more convincing than material dated no more closely than within a
century or two--as is the case with the vast majority of archaeological finds in Palestine to date.

Three things stand out as clearly objectionable. First is
excavation that does not follow methods capable of dating archaeological finds as closely as is presently possible. Sloppy digging
inevitably casts suspicion on proposed biblical connections. Second
is the forced correlation of archaeological material with what is
known from historical and biblical records. Many of the remains
of Mesad Hashavyahu fit well with historical considerations
suggesting occupation in the last third of the seventh century
B.C. A number of artifacts, however, have up to now been recovered
only from Persian contexts. The excavator's argument that these
forms must have originated in the seventh century is improper. The
forms suggest Persian occupants, as they do at all other sites--even
though such occupation is not attested in the meager written records.
Most objectionable is the attempt to use hypotheses as proof
of the accuracy or truth of the Bible. After all, an hypothesis
proves nothing--except that the final truth has not yet been achieved.
Archaeological hypotheses cannot legitimately serve as a foundation
or buttress for divine truth. From the perspective of chronology,
archaeology does not have sufficient precision to verify any biblical
statement as a fact--aside from extremely rare finds of histocial
documents.

Dating in Archaeology

Imagine that the world's first excavation was about to take
place in Palestine and you were the archaeologist. You proceded
to dig, carefully separating the artifacts from each layer. In
post-dig analysis you observed that frequently succeeding layers
seemed to contain a very similar repertory of forms, sometimes new
forms appeared alongside those of the preceding layer, and occasionally there were complete typal breaks between successive strata.
You were led to conclude that the groups separated by major breaks
in typology represented important chronological periods and that
new forms in basically similar groups represented innovations within the major periods.
This illustrates, in a simplified way, the two disciplines
that must be successfully employed if archaeological material is
to be closely dated--stratigraphy and typology. If layers are
mixed or if a pit is missed in digging, the typological analysis
will prove faulty. If the typological analysis does not concentrate on features distinguished by successive layers, it will not
be of chronological significance.
Archaeologists operate with relative and absolute dating.
The imagined succession of groups of artifacts by layer from the
first excavation in Palestine is in fact a relative chronology.
It provides evidence of forms which emerge, change, and disappear
at specific points in a sequence of layers representing human

habitation. In 1901 Sir Flinders Petrie, Palestine's first
scientific excavator, introduced the principle of sequence
dating. He attempted to reduce a mass of Egyptian tomb material
to fifty successive stages. These he designated SD 30-80, leaving
SD 1-29 for earlier cultures that might yet be discovered.
Material from early Palestinian digs was related to this relative
Egyptian sequence by Petrie and others. Thus Petrie's framework
was used as a means for combining the typological sequences from
the excavated sites and tombs of Palestine into a relative chronology.

How can relative chronology be converted into an absolute
B.C. or A.D. date? Suppose that in your first Palestinian excavation you had discovered three Ptolemaic coins of the early third
century B.C. on a floor. This would provide a good indication
that all groups of artifacts from layers below the floor predated
the coins and all subsequent layers postdated them. Nearly every
excavation adds a few such links with absolute chronology. When
the sequences from all excavations in Palestine are combined,
there are enough links with absolute chronology in most periods
to provide quite close absolute dates. As evidence from new digs
comes to light, the process of refining chronology continues.

From this perspective it might be expected that in its early
history Palestinian archaeology was geared to relative chronology,
and, as new evidence appeared, gradually more accurate absolute
dates were assigned to the successive phases. In fact the actual
progress toward precise absolute chronology in Palestinian archaeology took a much more confusing course. Progress followed a
circuitous route for many reasons.

Probably the chief block to orderly progress was the lack of
much careful, stratigraphic excavation all through the history of
Palestinian archaeology. Despite lack of precise stratigraphic
excavation methods, early excavators made progress in understanding the evolution of forms of artifacts, but these were thrown
into confusion by the seemingly reliable results of subsequent
digs. Finally in the 1930's more careful digging and publication
began introducing the sequential structure which still stands
today.

Another difficulty was the fact that from the start Palestinian
excavators tied their finds to the epochs and events of Near
Eastern history and archaeology. Once such relationships were
made, it became difficult to gain general assent for new proposals,
even when these had much stronger evidence behind them. This
situation needs interpretation in light of the fact that Palestinian excavators come out of the strong Western tradition of
independent research that often produces prima donna tendencies
among leading scholars. The failure of archaeologists to consider
the material of their colleagues, particularly those of another
nationality, before proposing or proclaiming their correlations is

by itself an important factor in the lack of steady progress toward chronological precision.

A third deterrent, particularly for the third and second millennia B.C., was the lack of consensus on the chronologies of Palestine's neighbors. Often the links between relative and absolute chronology consisted of imported artifacts from neighboring countries, where they were tied to the reign of a particular pharaoh or assigned a quite precise temporal span. Following Egyptian scholars, who plump for a high, a middle, or a low chronology for the early pharaohs, Palestinian scholars debate most often not the merits of each case, but which chronology best fits the material from Palestine. Such ad hoc arguments hardly contribute to advances in chronological precision.

A fourth detriment to systematic development of chronological precision was the neglect of detailed, critical pottery studies. Most scholars were content with knowledge of general lines of ceramic development based on oral tradition. These oral traditions were set down in the excavator's publications of his pottery. Newer pottery publications then cited or catalogued the previous examples of a particular pot along with proposed datings. Often no distinction was made between dates proposed for unstratified examples and for specimens from a context with good links to absolute chronology. This chorus of uncritical datings had the unfortunate result of gaining for the datings an undeserved confidence. If a dozen archaeologists cite a similar date for a certain form, it must be correct. Unfortunately, in many cases the dozen archaeologists were all merely repeating what was originally an uncritical oral tradition. Advances in chronological precision come when an archaeologist with a rigorously critical approach publishes a detailed study of the stratigraphic changes in ceramic forms and the evidence for their absolute dates.

Pottery Chronology

By far the most common finds on Palestinian tells are potsherds. Broken pieces of jars, jugs, bowls, and lamps litter virtually every layer of the mound from about 5000 B.C., when pottery first appeared in Palestine, down to modern times. In fact, many of the layers in the comparatively poor tells of Palestine contain nothing but sherds. If changes in pottery take place at a fairly rapid pace and can be identified, pottery can serve as the archaeologist's best chronological tool.

Pottery has many variable characteristics. Preparation of the clay includes levigating it to a coarser or smoother consistency and adding inclusions. The inclusions vary in fineness and consist of straw or grit of various kinds of stone or sand. The clay is formed into vessels by hand, on a slow or fast wheel, or in a mold, or a combination of these. The vessel may be shaved, decorated with incision or puncturing, surfaced with slip, paint, or glaze, and burnished or polished. It may be fired high or low in a kiln with or without reduction or stacking. Further decorative wash, burnishing, or incision may be executed after firing.

Nearly all of these features are of at least potential chronological significance. Pottery from one era of a town's history may have used different clay beds than their predecessors, used different inclusions, preferred incision to painted decoration, fired their kilns higher, and the like. Some features offer rather precise chronological indications. For instance, pattern burnishing was in vogue only for a few brief periods of Palestine's history, and overfiring of pots was common in the later Late Bronze age and the Early Hellenistic period. Spectographic analysis and careful attention to inclusions would provide helpful results for chronology, but the analysis is expensive and time-consuming and will be of little significance until such analysis is consistently reported by a number of excavations.

While these characteristics offer chronological data, only rarely do they reach the level of chronological precision required if archaeological material is to be of historical value. The same clay beds, potters' wheels, and painted traditions often lasted for centuries. There is only one feature of ceramic vessels that undergoes a continuous process of change that can be observed at intervals of a quarter- or half-century. That feature is shape.

The most common categories of ancient ceramic vessels are jars, jugs, juglets, craters, bowls, cups, platters, cooking pots, and lamps. In the Early Bronze age, for example, there may be several jar types but perhaps only one jug type. Some jar types continue through the Early Bronze age; others may be introduced at an early stage and disappear at a late stage within the Early Bronze age. These are chronological facts of significance, but what is of importance for precise chronology is the change that takes place in the shape of a particular jar type during the course of the Early Bronze age. Bases may become more pointed, rounded, flattened, or elongated. Handles may shift their point of attachment, change their manner of attachment, or develop from round to oval to flat. Most often rims are the best chronological indicators. Possible rim shapes are almost infinite, and a particular rim shape tends to develop persistently and rapidly. Such changes in shape are perhaps the closest counterparts to the modern phenomenon of annual model changes for cars and appliances.

To leave the impression that all pots change shape regularly and rapidly would be incorrect. Some shapes tend to change much more rapidly than others. Jar rims tend to be much more precise chronological indicators than lamps. Some forms seem to persist for centuries with little or no change, while other types disappear after flourishing for only a few years or decades. A few simple

types tend to persist or recur century after century. Some
exotic shapes have a very short life and can be immediately
identified and closely dated even by a novice.

For those schooled in an "evolutionary mentality," it
should be noted that the formal trend of Palestinian--and
indeed all ancient pottery is commonly downward. Finely made
examples of a new and pleasing shape appear. Soon a decline in
quality becomes apparent and the shape begins to sag or bulge.
Since it is virtually impossible to accurately publish subtle
changes in quality even by verbal description, a refined understanding of the dating of pots requires extensive experience in
going over basket after basket of pottery as it comes from layer
after layer in the field.

The knowledge of pottery chronology grew as leading excavators
such as Sir Flinders Petrie, Père L.-H. Vincent, and Clarence
Fisher shared their field observations. The critical examination
of this oral tradition and the publication of normative ceramic
groups issued from the digging of W. F. Albright at Tell Beit
Mirsim in southern Judea. In the final reports of that excavation, published between 1932 and 1943, Albright was able to provide a fairly complete picture of the changes in pottery shapes
from the late third millennium down to the early sixth century
B.C.[1] Pottery chronology for the periods preceding Tell Beit
Mirsim was systematized in a dissertation under Albright's
direction by G. Ernest Wright in 1937.[2] Systematization of our
knowledge of pottery chronology for later periods has been slow
to appear. The writer's dissertaion, published in 1961, attempted
to systematize the ceramic chronology for the period from 200 B.C.
to A.D. 70.[3] Well-dated material for the late fourth and third
centuries B.C. has been recently published by Fawzi Zayadine and
Nancy Lapp,[4] and the first published attempt to define the formal
changes of the Persian period is found in my contribution to the
Kurt Galling Festschrift, issued in 1970.[5] Knowledge of pottery
development in the periods after A.D. 70 is still confined largely
to a quite imprecise oral tradition.[6]

The constant stream of newly published material has made
possible considerable refinement of the chronologies of Wright
and Albright. Among the most notable of these are Basil Hennessy's
study of the Early Bronze age, Kathleen Kenyon's analysis of the
Bronze age tombs at Jericho, and the publication of the Iron age
pottery of Samaria by Kenyon and of Tell Deir 'Alla by H. K.
Franken.[7] In our present state of refinement, and with few
exceptions, we are able to date larger ceramic groups from the
late fourth millennium B.C. through the first century A.D. within
a century. In many instances in the last two millennia B.C. it
is possible to date groups within fifty years, and on occasion
within a quarter-century.

It should be apparent that an expert in ceramic chronology is
indispensible for any dig dealing with post-5000 B.C. material in

Palestine. In most cases pottery provides the crucial and exclusive evidence for dating the dig's discoveries. If this evidence is not controlled, the finds of a dig are of little more significance than those purchased in an antique shop. In fact, if an excavator does not have a thorough knowledge of ceramic chronology, he would be favoring historians if he were to stop digging and purchase his artifacts from an antiquities dealer.

Other Dating Aids

Before the introduction of pottery about 5000 B.C., the most ubiquitous stratified finds are flints. While they provide the best evidence available, they do not provide as precise chronological indications as pottery. Once introduced, a flint type tends to persist longer than a pottery type, but without any developments comparable to those of pot rims, handles, and bases. This means that our chronological knowledge is much less precise, and, in fact, the farther into the past we penetrate, the longer are the periods we are able to identify.

The resulting picture is usually interpreted as an indication that the farther back we go, the slower was the pace of change and development. This interpretation should be accepted with some skepticism, for the picture is actually the result of a lack of materials for delimiting shorter periods of time. Time and again new evidence from pre-history has astounded even the specialists with its sophistication. The third millennium B.C. is still commonly called the horizon of Palestine's earliest towns, but the Jericho excavations have brought to light a massively fortified town of the seventh millennium B.C. The sophistication of its houses is sufficient to emphasize that periods of creative development were heavily interspersed with eras of stagnation. Some earlier ages may have changed as rapidly as those where pottery makes the changes perceptible.

Technically speaking recorded history begins about 3200 B.C., the date of the Sumerian documents bearing man's earliest known writing. By the early third millennium B.C. the archaeological materials of Palestine can be linked with the absolute dates derived from the early documents of her neighbors. Until recently prehistoric material was largely confined to sequence dating. Archaeologists may have rather arbitrarily estimated how long certain changes took or relied on the extremely broad datings of palaeontologists, among whom disagreements over periods of five million years are not uncommon.

Much greater precision has been achieved in prehistoric chronology through Carbon 14 dating. Carbon 14 is a radioactive isotope of carbon with a half life adjusted in 1962 to 5730 $\pm$ 40 years. Most available dates were figured from the previously accepted half life of 5568 ± 30 years. Others have operated with a half life of 5800 years.

This range of over 200 years in half life determination is already an indication of the relative precision of Carbon 14 dates. To be added to this is a ± factor, usually expressed as a 1 value. With a 1 value the chances are one in three that the actual date lies beyond the proposed date range. It would seem preferable to work with a 2 tolerance in which chances are 21 in 22 of the date falling within the proposed range. This would put dates about 3000 B.C. in a ± 250 year range, 6000 B.C. dates in a ± 500 year range, and earlier dates with a correspondingly larger tolerance factor. Carbon 14 dating is still in process of refinement. Its dates will perhaps require additional slight adjustments, but it has already introduced considerable clarity into the chronology of the later prehistoric periods. Its chief limitations are the necessity of a relatively large sample of carbonized material for destruction and the cost of $100 to $250 per test.[8]

It is a common misconception that Carbon 14 has also made important contributions to chronological precision in the historical period. From the third millennium B.C. on Carbon 14 dates can do no more than corroborate in a very general way the datings derived from the study of pottery and other artifacts. If pottery from a certain stratum points to a date in the first half of the sixteenth century B.C., it is reassuring to have a 2 Carbon 14 date of 1720 ± 175 B.C. On the other hand, if the Carbon 14 date came out 1257 ± 160 B.C., it should more than likely be dismissed as a contaminated sample. Carbon 14 dating is not precise enough to contribute to chronological precision in the historical period.

Compared with pots most other kinds of artifacts are relatively poor chronological indicators. They do not occur frequently enough in stratum after stratum to provide the constant chronological indication needed by the field archaeologist. Their sparsity has also meant a lack of sufficient stratified evidence to define rapid typological changes that might exist in certain categories of artifacts.

Stone vessels and implements are notoriously conservative. Millstones and grinding bowls persist for centuries and millennia with no apparent change of form. Occasional groups, such as the Hyksos alabasters, can be associated with a particular period, but even in such cases I know of no uninscribed stone vessels that can be dated to any single century with confidence. Fashions in metal tools and weapons changed more rapidly, but no particular specimen can be dated within a century. Blown glass, first appearing in the Early Roman period, is limited by its technique to a fairly small typological repertory and is of similarly limited chronological value.

Finds of clothing fasteners and jewelry of all kinds are still less common, so that characteristics only of broader periods may be identified. Jewelry confronts us with other chronological complications inherent in individual taste, international style, and especially the heirloom factor. Jewelry may be preserved in royal and aristocratic families for centuries. Figurines, including the relatively common fertility goddesses, have similar chronological limitations, enforced by the conservative tendencies of superstition.

Scarabs can on occasion serve as links with absolute chronology when they bear the symbols of one of the pharaohs. Unfortunately carving of scarabs bearing a pharaoh's fame often continued long after his death. As a result, the manner in which the carver portrayed the beetle is often of more chronological importance than the symbols carved on its belly. Recent publications of groups of hundreds of scarabs, such as those from the Jericho tombs, are disappointing from a chronological perspective.

Seals, too, on occasion serve as links with absolute chronology when they bear the name of a known ruler or official. Even when they bear unknown names, their script can often be quite closely dated. Seals belong to artistic styles which can at times be dated within a century. If seals were as common as potsherds on Palestinian mounds, our chronological framework would be much more precise. Unfortunately they are rather rare finds in the poor mounds of Palestine.

Coins first appear in Palestine about 500 B.C. and become common after the fourth century B.C. Since most coins can be attributed to a particular ruler and often indicate a specific year of his reign, they are of considerable importance as chronological indicators and as links with absolute chronology. Perhaps the main reason for the comparative neglect of pottery chronology after the sixth century B.C. is the assumption that coins can replace potsherds as chronological indicators in the later periods. This premise is wrong for a number of reasons. While coins are rather common finds, they are far less ubiquitous than potsherds. Many later layers of Palestinian mounds contain no coins. Since coins are small, they often present stratigraphic problems. Has this coin slipped through a crack into a lower layer? Was this coin on the floor or in the fill immediately above? Even hoards of coins may present stratigraphic difficulties for they are frequently hidden in cracks and crevices. Most important is the heirloom factor. Coins remained in circulation in antiquity longer than they do at present with the popularity of coin collecting. When a single coin is found on a floor, it is impossible to tell for sure it was minted a few years, several decades, or even a century before it was lost.

Where ceramic chronology has not been precisely worked out, numismatic evidence often provides the best chronological data.

Where groups of pots can be dated within a quarter- or half-
century, coin evidence often provides no more than general cor-
roboration of the ceramic dating. The endurance of common
crockery for a half century or more would be quite exceptional,
but quite common for coins. Perhaps it sounds unbelievable that
uninscribed sherds can serve as better chronological indicators
than dated coins, but this is often the case.

We have noted that some more or less precise links with
absolute chronology are provided by Carbon 14 dates, scarabs,
seals, and coins. The two chief sources of chronological links
in Bronze and Iron age Palestine are written material and imports.
Subsequently, in the third century B.C., coins become a third
common source.

As already noted, shorter inscriptions are often found on
scarabs, seals, and coins. Occasionally a pot will be incised
with the name of its owner or potter. Monumental inscriptions
are found on standing stones or stele, on statue bases, and on
the walls and floors of buildings. All such written material may
be classed as incised because its letters are ordinarily carved.
Related are the clay tablets inscribed in the cuneiform characters
of the Mesopotamians by a wedge-headed stylus. Documents written
in ink are less often preserved, but such recent discoveries as
the Dead Sea Scrolls, the Samaria Papyri, and the Arad ostraca are
spectacular examples of the preservation of such documents in
Palestine. Most of the Dead Sea Scrolls are parchments, written
on specially treated animal skins prepared in long rolls. Papyrus
sheets are prepared by weaving strips of the papyrus reed. An
ostracon is a potsherd which served as a piece of scratch paper,
for short messages, receipts, bills of lading, and the like.

Written finds are even more infrequent than in neighboring
lands, and documents bearing a date are rare among written finds.
Not a single specific date is mentioned in the Dead Sea Scrolls,
but each of the Samaria papyri bore the day, month, and year of
writing. The writers, of course, were not aware of how many
years before Christ they lived, but the years of the reign of a
particular Persian king are easily converted into B.C. dates.

Even when documents bear no dates, they are usually of considerable chronological help. This is because handwriting changes
about as rapidly as the shapes of pots and can be closely dated.
Even though the Dead Sea Scrolls bear no dates, the evolution of
the script of the first centuries B.C. and A.D. makes possible
the dating of individual documents to a quarter- or half-century.
It should be emphasized that just as the inscriptions on contemporary buildings differ from our handwriting, so it is
necessary to distinguish between the development of ancient
incised and cursive scripts. Cursive writing tends to change
much more rapidly.

For the last three millennium B.C. the most common finds
providing links with absolute chronology are imports, mostly

pottery. Often the pots imported into Palestine from Egypt, Cyprus, Greece, Phoenicia, Syria, Anatolia, Mesopotamia, and even farther abroad can be assigned quite precise absolute dates in their countries of manufacture. Discounting a short time lag for shipment, these dates may be accepted as manufacturing dates for the examples found in Palestine.

It should be emphasized that the date indicated by the imported pot is its date of manufacture, and the date indicated by a script is the date the document was written or the artifact was inscribed. This does not mean that these dates can automatically be applied to the strata in which they are found. If they indicate a date in agreement with that provided by the local potsherds with which they are found, they corroborate that date. They may well date earlier than the ceramic horizon with which they were found. Dead Sea Scrolls from a single cave may be dated from the late third century B.C. to the middle of the first century A.D. Imported pots may have been used rarely and been preserved much longer than local kitchen ware, just as our "good china" is often much older than our "everyday dishes". Written documents and imports, like coins, are often subject to the heirloom factor. On the other hand, if the date provided by the import or written material postdates the ceramic horizon of the layer, something is wrong with the dating of the pot in its country of origin, the dating of the script, the local ceramic chronology, or, most commonly, the stratigraphic excavation or analysis.

A very rare link with absolute chronology is provided when constructions specifically described in historical texts can be located. The most dramatic example of this for Palestine is a discovery of Yigael Yadin. After excavating a gateway from the time of Solomon at Hazor, he noted gateways with virtually identical plan and dimension at Megiddo and Gezer. That all three were in fact planned by Solomon's architect is confirmed by the biblical account, "This is an account of the forced labor King Solomon levied for the building of...the wall of Jerusalem, Hazor, Megiddo, and Gezer" (I Kings 9:15). This means that the pottery contemporary with the construction of these defenses may be assigned with considerable confidence to the reign of Solomon. Even such discoveries contribute less to the refinement of ceramic chronology than might be expected. Unfortunately, none of the three gateways have been excavated according to the best stratigraphic methods.

Chronology on a Dig

On a dig in Palestine archaeologists get up early. Work begins at 5 or 6 a.m. so that heavy labor will be completed before the heat of the day, in conformity with practical local tradition.

At times the archaeologist finds it necessary to begin his day
even before the diggers. He may want to be sure that a crucial
floor or wall is photographed in the soft light of dawn before
it is destroyed when work begins. He may need to check the
drawing of a balk section before it is removed or before the sun
washes out the lines of the layers. The pottery study of the
previous evening may have suggested that a pit was being missed,
and he wants to help locate and define it before it contaminates
any more digging.

Early in the workday the director-archaeologist makes a tour
of the mound. In each excavation theater he discusses with the
supervisor plans for the day's digging, problems in tracing or
relating the layers under excavation, new or interesting finds
since the last visit, problems or conclusions reached in studying
the pottery of the theater the night before, and such practical
problems as how meticulously the layers should be dug, how most
effectively to deploy the laborers, and the placement of dump.
This tour may consume much of the first half of the labor day,
and he rushes back to his desk to record the impressions from
his tour and deal with such inevitable problems as hiring and
firing.

After "second breakfast" the second half of the work day finds
him examining the artifacts coming from the field, giving an eye
to the washing and laying out of pottery, checking the quality of
field and object photographs, consulting with the architect on his
plans, and answering emergency calls from the field. After a
second, and usually briefer, tour of the mound, there may be time
to examine some of the potsherds with a supervisor or two before
the work day ends and the midday meal is served about 2 p.m.
After a siesta or quiet reading the staff puts in a couple of
hours on the mound completing the daily plans of their squares,
drawing sections, studying stratigraphy, or preparing for photography. The archaeologist joins them where required to discuss
the drawings, sections, stratigraphy, and may take pictures or
superintend the photography.

After supper he has a two or three hour schedule of "pottery
reading". He examines the potsherds with the supervisor who
details their layer by layer description. Each basket of pottery
from every layer is examined separately. Whole vessels are
encountered rarely; most of them come from tombs. But a characteristic sherd is enough to bring the entire form to the mind's
eye of a skilled archaeologist. In mixed fills and other loci
with pottery from more than one horizon or chronological period
he attempts to note the periods represented, paying special
attention to the dating of the latest sherds. In the less common
homogeneous pottery baskets, such as should come from floor or
destruction debris he is on the lookout for intrusive sherds of
other periods, indicating error in the digging or processing of

the sherds. He selects sherds to be saved for their unique features, to substantiate his dating analysis, and especially those that may prove desirable for publication.

By the end of the pottery session the supervisor has a rather precise dating for the layers he is digging. As his evidence accumulates he is able to organize his layers into a stratum. A stratum may be defined as all those layers, disturbances, and installations that can be associated with a single continuous period of occupation. Then he will be able to see the relation of his portion of the stratum to that being unearthed in adjoining areas. With visions of stratum plans and pot forms dancing through their heads, the archaeologist and his staff retire for the night. Nightmares have to do with that wall for which there was insufficient pottery evidence for close dating, that pit that has defied detection for three days, and the failure to separate the loose gray layer from the soft gray one.[9]

Whether it follows the pattern just described or another, virtually all the archaeologist's tasks are oriented toward dating his discoveries as precisely as possible. Much of his time is devoted to stratigraphic excavation, to clean digging and concise recording of each successive layer of earth and its contents. Why? So that each excavated element can be dated as closely as the evidence from it will permit. The considerable time he devotes to his finds, especially pottery, is rewarded if he is able to produce a reliable typological sequence and validate for it a precise structure of absolute dates. Concern for accuracy, detail, and completeness in plans, sections, photographs, and artifact drawings is required if the precise details of chronological development of buildings and defenses, pots and jewelry, ovens and basins are to be understood, communicated, and fit into Palestine's chronological and typological structures. Even firing is often necessitated by the inability of a pickman to lightly pick one layer at a time, of a hoeman to carefully separate out his sherds, or of a basket carrier to keep apart pottery from separate layers.

What about the many excavations where attention in the field is not focused on precise digging and dating? Such digs tend to fall into three classes. First, there are those excavations that are content with older and less exacting methods of excavation and a general knowledge of pottery chronology. Some of these excavators even ridicule the possibility of very precise dating. Their conclusions are either too imprecise to be of much value to the historian or they jump at biblical or historical connections inappropriate for their broadly dated material.

A second category of digs attempts to employ precise methods of stratigraphic digging and recording. In fact, this effort consumes so much of the time and energy of the staff that little time is left for studying the finds being unearthed while the dig

is in progress. The potsherds are all carefully labelled and
put in accurately tagged bags for future study. All digs follow
the pattern of sorting and saving material for more definitive
future study, so what is the advantage to preliminary study in
the field? Considerable! It has already been described how
daily examination of the pottery serves as a corrective in
stratigraphic excavation in pointing to such mistakes as over-
looked pits. Basically the advantage is that the precise interpretation of the excavation is the result of a working hypothesis
that has been subject to development, correction, and refinement
by those working with the evidence in the field. When the materials
are studied by one man or even a team of researchers after excavation, questions will arise for which the records will not preserve
answers. In the field such answers can be obtained before the
evidence is destroyed by excavation. Hypotheses developed in the
field and refined thereafter are inevitably more valid and reliable
than those with details constructed from carefully bagged samples.

A final class of excavations employs sloppy digging methods
but gives meticulous attention to the finds. A thorough knowledge
of comparative typology produces confidence that excavation
elements can be precisely dated even when all the layers are not
dug separately and when the pits and intrusions have not been
carefully isolated. Intrusive material can be easily eliminated,
and a chronologically homogeneous group of potsherds and artifacts
can be quickly assembled and published as representing a particular
stratum. Such publication provides valuable evidence on the occupational history of the site, but it is impossible to give any
individual stratigraphic element a precise date. In fact, many of
the individual elements are not even defined by publication of
detailed sections. This means basically that such digs impose
stratigraphical and typological results from other sites upon their
material without really defining empirically the stratigraphy of
their own site.

If we return to the rather awkward characterization of the
relation of an excavator to his ruin as a love affair, the excavation finds can be considered the offspring of the relationship.
The responsible archaeologist is not only in love with his mound
but shows tender loving care for everything it produces. This
includes doing his best to understand the offspring on its own
terms, in its own context, with as precise a dating as possible.
It is this consideration that determines the pace of an excavation.
Like lovers, some archaeologists dig their mounds too slowly, others
spoil the relationship by digging too fast. The best field archaeologist digs as fast as he can without sacrificing chronological
precision.

Palestine's Chronological Structure[10]

In 1961 G. E. Wright presented a concise survey of the
archaeology of Palestine from Mesolithic to Iron II times
complete with chronological tables showing the stratified
material from sites known to that time.[11] Since then a vast
amount of new material has come to light. The chronological
table published here attempts to take new material into consideration. The table may then serve as a reference for the
remaining chapters and other Palestinian archaeological and
historical material the reader may consult. A few remarks are
needed.

The standard survey of the archaeology of Palestine for the
Neolithic through the Early Bronze age is that of R. de Vaux in
the Revised Edition of the Cambridge Ancient History.[12] Wright
accepted these studies in general, but in a review article in
1971 discussed differences and new data.[13] In our table Wright's
classification and terminology is generally followed for the pre-
Early Bronze period.[14] For the Early Bronze period the dates
follow Paul Lapp's correlations shortly before his death with
slight alterations presented by R. T. Schaub in his dissertation
and in further study of the Bab edh-Dhrâ' material and the latest
radio carbon and Suess bristlecone pine calibration.[15] The discussion of the controversial Early Bronze IV and Middle Bronze I
periods was conveniently summarized by W. Dever in 1973, drawing
heavily upon Schaub's study of the Bab edh-Dhrâ' Early Bronze IV
material.[16]

For the Middle Bronze age Wright's designations are accepted,
which he based principally on his unpublished work at Shechem.[17]
The dates for the Late Bronze age are correlated with the Eighteenth
and Nineteenth Egyptian Dynasties, a period of Egyptian dominance
in Palestine.[18] Iron I and Iron II dates are generally those of
Albright and Wright,[19] with the exception that the division between
Iron II A and B is placed at about 722 B.C., the fall of the
Northern Kingdom, since that event caused major changes at many
sites (new archaeological strata appear) and because of the many
sites which have narrowly defined late Iron II deposits.[20]

With the fall of the Southern Kingdom many archaeological
surveys have ended in Palestine.[21] The post-587 B.C. chronological framework presented here is largely the result of the research
of the writer and her husband. It should be noted that the terminology from this point on is historical, rather than the cultur-
ally-related terms--bronze, iron, copper, and stone.

The first stratigraphical typological division of the 587-
332 B.C. period was made by P. W. Lapp in his article in the
Galling Festschrift in 1970.[22] He designated the entire period
as "Persian," but in reality the Persians were not part of the
historical picture of Palestine until 539 B.C.--after the conquests

of Cyrus the Great and the return from the Babylonian exile. I
have therefore chosen to call the period 587-539 B.C., "Exilic".[23]
P. W. Lapp suggested 480 B.C. as a division between Early and
Late Persian,[24] and further study of Persian pottery has justified
this.

For the Hellenistic and Roman periods the terminology of
P. W. Lapp in <u>Palestinian Ceramic Chronology</u>, <u>200 B.C.-A.D. 70</u> may
be noted,[25] and his designations are adopted here. For the later
periods J. Sauer has outlined a comprehensive system as a result
of his study of the Hesbon pottery.[26] A simplified form for the
Byzantine and Islamic periods is presented here in the hope that
further studies will refine the terminology suggested.

PALESTINIAN CHRONOLOGY

ca. 2 million years ago		PALEOLITHIC	"Old Stone Age" (Pleistocene)

ca. 10,000 B.C.   MESOLITHIC   "Middle Stone Age"
         (Natufian)

ca. 8,000 - 4300   NEOLITHIC   "New Stone Age"
         8000   Pre-pottery
         7000   (Tahunian)
         6000   Pottery

ca. 4300 - 3200   CHALCOLITHIC   "Copper Age"
         4300   Early
               (Yarmukian)
         3600   Late
               (Ghassulian)

ca. 3200 - 2050   EARLY BRONZE
         3200   I A = Kenyon's Proto-Urban A
               I B = Kenyon's Proto-Urban B
               I C = Kenyon's EB I
         2850   II
         2550   III
         2300   IV = Intermediate Bronze I ⎫
                                      ⎬ Kenyon's
ca. 2050 - 1550   MIDDLE BRONZE   = Intermediate
         2050   I = Intermediate Bronze II ⎭ EB-MB
         1900   II A = Kenyon's MB I
         1750   II B
         1650   II C

ca. 1550 - 1200   LATE BRONZE
         1550   I
         1400   II A
         1300   II B

ca. 1200 - 918   IRON I
         1200   A
         1150   B
         1000   C

ca. 918 - 587   IRON II
         918   A
         722   B

587 - 539   EXILIC

PALESTINIAN CHRONOLOGY
(continued)

539 - 332		PERSIAN
	539	Early
	480	Late
332 - 63		HELLENISTIC
	332	Early (Ptolemaic)
	198	Late (Seleucid)
	167	(Hasmonian)
63 B.C. - A.D. 324		ROMAN
	63	Early
		(Herodian 37 - 4 B.C.)
		(Fall of Jerusalem A.D. 70)
	A.D. 135	Late
		(Second Jewish Revolt A.D. 135)
A.D. 324 - 630		BYZANTINE
	324	Early
		(Constantine I 324 - 337)
	491	Late
		(Justinian I 527 - 565)
630 - 1516		ARABIC/ISLAMIC
		(Muhammed 630)
	661	Umayyad
	750	Abbasid
	969	Fatimid
		(Crusades 1099 - 1291)
	1174	Ayyubid
	1250	Mamluk
1516 - 1918		TURKISH/OTTOMAN
1918 - 1948		MANDATE
1948 - present		ISRAEL/JORDAN

Chapter IV

PALESTINE: KNOWN BUT MOSTLY UNKNOWN[1]

Palestine is perhaps the most excavated land in the world.
Certainly the archaeological history of no country is better
known. Since the beginning of archaeological work in Palestine
at Tell el-Hesī in 1890 there have been few periods when there
were not several expeditions in the field. The most complete
survey of current archaeological work in Palestine is the
"Chronique" of the Revue Biblique. The 1962 "Chronique" mentions
nearly fifty sites at which archaeological discoveries were
reported, mainly in 1960 and 1961. More than half these sites
have been subjected to substantial excavation.

How Much Do We Know?

With some knowledge of the scope of archaeological activity
in Palestine visitors in Jerusalem frequently ask: Are there still
new sites to dig? Are there still exciting finds to be made in
Palestine? One might go on to ask: Isn't our knowledge of biblical times fairly complete? Don't we have a picture of daily life
at the time of Jesus which can be modified only in detail by
future discoveries? The confidence with which archaeological conclusions are frequently drawn and the long books devoted to daily
life in Palestine at the time of Jesus might suggest an affirmative
answer.

My viewpoint here is that such a tiny fraction of the archaeological material has been excavated, and such a small fraction
of that satisfactorily published, that even the most assured archaeological conclusions must still be considered far from final.
This does not mean that all archaeological conclusions must be
basically vague and noncommittal. Our knowledge of Palestinian
archaeology has been built step by step, from the best hypothesis
explaining evidence available at an early stage of exploration to
the best hypothesis to explain evidence currently at hand. Without
the discipline of continuous updating of hypotheses as new evidence
comes to light chaos would prevail. The nonspecialist would find
it much more difficult to judge among interpretations than is now
the case. All that is stressed here is that in view of the vast
amount of unknown material, archaeologists will be forced to
modify or reformulate many, if not all, their hypotheses regarding
the development of Palestine as the flood of new evidence continues
to grow. Palestinian archaeology may be past infancy but has
hardly gotten beyond childhood.

There are some 5,000 recorded antiquities sites and monuments
in Palestine and Transjordan. Supplement No. 2 to the Palestine

Gazette Extraordinary No. 1375 of 24 November, 1944 listed some
3,500 spots as coming under the provisions of the then effective
Antiquities Ordinance. Nelson Glueck has dealt with well over a
thousand sites in Transjordan, and this study was not entirely
comprehensive.[2] If the new sites among the 400 in the Negeb
examined by Glueck,[3] and other sites more recently discovered,
are added, a total of approximately 5,000 sites is reached.

Even this number will be steadily, though not rapidly,
increased from year to year. This year, for example, the American
School in Jerusalem has just excavated in two cemeteries north of
'Ain Sāmiyeh (Pl. 11).[4] Neither of these had been listed as archaeological sites, and at least three other unrecorded cemeteries
have been noted in the vicinity. The cave in the Wâdī ed-Dâliyeh
from which the Samaria Papyri were recovered (Pls. 7 and 8) and
the nearby cave inhabited in the Middle Bronze I period had not
been previously noted.[5] The annual topographical studies by members
of the German Evangelical Institute usually bring to light yet unrecorded sites, and this year was no exception.

Scientific excavations, including small soundings and
clearances, have taken place at some 150 sites, or about three in
a hundred. The Westminster Historical Atlas to the Bible (1956),
plate 18, records nearly a hundred excavated sites, and the total
recorded in the Oxford Bible Atlas, page 96 (to 1958), is some
forty higher. Of these, the Westminster Atlas records major excavations at 26 sites, the Oxford Atlas at fifteen. This means
that roughly one site in 200 has been the scene of major archaeological work. To be sure, many of the sites on record would not
merit extensive excavation, but if only one in four were promising,
major excavations have till now been carried out at only two per
cent of the potential sites.

More or less adequate records of surface finds and extant
monuments exist for the recorded sites mentioned here, especially
those in Transjordan and the Negeb studied by Nelson Glueck. Substantial historical conclusions may be drawn from this mass of
evidence from surface exploration, but arguments from silence are
always dangerous when dealing with this material, even when minor
excavation has been carried out. At 'Arâq el-Emîr, for example,
surface exploration failed to recover any evidence of Iron I
occupation, and yet excavation exposed impressive remnants of an
Iron I fort. In a first campaign two five-meter squares were excavated to bedrock, but it was not until the second season that
any evidence of occupation in the Chalcolithic and Early Bronze
periods came to light. Even after three campaigns only a few
sherds and coins purchased from the villagers suggest that Persian
and Early Hellenistic stratification, the excavator's main concern,
may yet appear in a future campaign.

As the home of Amos, Tekoa has attracted many visitors in
Palestine with biblical interests. The visitor will hardly forget
the barren, rocky mound with hardly enough dirt covering it to

justify much of an excavation. Today convincing evidence of
Middle Bronze II tombs appeared. Yesterday beautiful Middle
Bronze I pots from there were offered for sale in Jerusalem.
Two weeks ago I visited the site to record the tomb from which
a beautiful seventh century B.C. tomb group was taken, and while
there Architect David Voelter was able to plan an Early Roman
tomb just discovered during the building of a new house (by
Taʿâmireh bedouin with money they earned from manuscript
purchases). Obviously this site is ripe for a major tomb search
and excavation project. Tekoa and ʿArâq el-Emîr are just two
current examples of the wealth of material which might be await-
ing the excavator at any one of 5,000 sites--of which there may
be no hint in surface exploration records.

True, one may think, but certainly the chief biblical sites
and the richest and most promising areas have already been excavated. This is true only to a small degree. A number of
important biblical sites are still untouched, Jabesh-gilead, Ramah
and Hebron, for instance. Two of the host of untouched spots with
minor biblical connections, Tell ed-Dâmiyeh (biblical Adamah) and
Qarn Sarṭabeh (Herod the Great's Alexandrium), may be noted. Many
ancient cities and villages have been disturbed only slightly by
excavations. Bethlehem, Bethel, and Bethany are among these.
Especially to be emphasized is the fact that at every site of a
major excavation much more remains for the future than has been
so far unearthed. The area dug during the three current seasons
at Jerusalem added to that disturbed by almost countless past
expeditions together accounts for only a tiny fraction of the
surface of historical Jerusalem. Even Jericho, one of the most
fully excavated sites in Palestine, could still keep a large
expedition busy for many years. In fact, Miss Kenyon has planned
her excavations so that substantial portions of the tell will
remain available for future excavations when archaeological
methodology has been improved and new techniques and analyses
developed and refined. Only at Megiddo was there an attempt to
strip a tell layer by layer, and there the plan was soon abandoned.

There need be little fear that the constant flood of new and
interesting artifacts coming to light through excavation and
appearing in antiquities shops will begin to ebb in the foreseeable
future. "Flood" is hardly an exaggeration. In the past two
months on the Jordan side of Palestine, besides the Tekoa finds,
the Jerusalem excavation has turned up enough inscribed Hebrew
weights to double our evidence on the subject; the Taanach expedition has unearthed several hundred artifacts in a cult context
(Pl. 20) including a unique Astarte figurine mold (Pl. 21), plus a
Canaanite cuneiform tablet providing the best evidence yet on
writing in twelfth century B.C. Palestine; Roman tombs in Jerusalem
have produced spectacular jewelry and one of the finest collections
of bone pins known; the richest Late Bronze burials yet discovered

in Palestine have been excavated at Pella; some 35 Middle Bronze
I tomb plans have been recorded at Dhahr Mirzbâneh, several with
large intact tomb groups (Pl. 14); important structures and
ostraca of the first and second century A.D. are reported from
Herodium; important finds in a sounding at Shiloh have led to
plans for resuming major work there; topographical work has led
to a number of cogent new identifications of biblical and historical sites; and, as usual, more ancient documents are appearing on
the market. News reports indicate that comparable discoveries
have been taking place in Israel within the same period.

A Coordinated Strategy?

The last paragraph might give the impression that the flood
of evidence pouring in is rather spontaneous and quite uncontrolled.
Such an impression is perfectly correct. Apart from the practically
complete lack of contact between archaeologists working in Israel
and those digging in Jordan, there is practically no coordination
of excavation aims or plans between and among the separate expeditions. The Departments of Antiquities have no schedules of the
ten most crucial sites in need of excavation. Responsible expeditions are free to select a site of their choice, and, unless there
are other claims on the site, a license can usually be obtained
without difficulty. In Jordan competent American expeditions
usually seek association with the American Schools of Oriental
Research, but expeditions failing to meet its standards have
little difficulty obtaining excavation permits. Indeed, recently
royal patronage has been secured for such projects as the quest
for the treasures mentioned in the Copper Scroll from Qumrân Cave 3,
diving for the cities of Sodom and Gomorrah under the Dead Sea, and
a search for the body of Moses.[6]
Interested persons with an orderly frame of mind have often
asked how a more systematic program of excavation could be introduced, and archaeologist colleagues have discussed coordination of
the activities of the Departments of Antiquities and the various
archaeological schools at work in Palestine. Some countries such
as Turkey are quite strict about granting permits, and the choice
of sites is quite limited in terms of the resources and plans of
the expedition and the long term plans for its archaeological sites
by the Department of Antiquities. To be sure, permission to excavate in Palestine should be based on such conditions as demonstra-
tion of a competent staff, evidence of resources adequate to carry
on an excavation in keeping with the nature of the site, and
assurance of high standard scholarly publication. Certainly no
excavation should be licensed without a carefully trained and
experienced archaeologist. Beyond this is a long range or
coordinated program of excavation possible or desirable?

Underlying an answer to this question is the observation that
it is impossible to provide satisfactory solutions to most of the
problems of archaeologists concerned with history either by excavating according to the principle of random sample or by a calcu-
lated study of surface and literary evidence. If you were an
archaeologist interested in gathering evidence on cult practices
in the Early Bronze age, you might wish to put the names of sites
at which Early Bronze sherds occur in a hat and select three at
random. Chances are good that one of the sites is covered with
masses of Byzantine and Roman debris, another is the site of a
modern village, and the third is located where there is not an
adequate labor force or water supply. In any case, excavators are
not usually in a position to consider work at more than one site
at a time, and if they have funds in hand for the next season, they
consider themselves fortunate.

If, on the other hand, you studied each Early Bronze tell with
care, were well acquainted with all pertinent material excavated
in Palestine and neighboring lands, and came to the conclusion
that precisely this spot on this mound is the most promising in
Palestine for recovering Early Bronze cult material, most experienced
Palestinian archaeologists would probably offer generous odds against
your finding what you were looking for. Perhaps what you seek will
remain hidden a few feet from your excavation; perhaps cult remains
had been entirely razed in the later occupational history of the
tell; perhaps this site had no special cult area. Even if you were
to discover clear cult remains, could these be considered a representative find or could they represent a unique pilgrimage center
or the seat of a wizard with his own ideas? In this instance, as
in many similar problems, there is hardly enough comparative
material to decide what could be considered typical or representative.

Under these circumstances most larger excavations in Palestine
approach a mound with a series of aims and objectives and are open
to the responsibilities of careful excavation and publication of
whatever the pick brings up. These aims are such that only one or
a few mounds may be considered completely satisfactory for a given
expedition. An expedition digging for the first time in Jordan
this summer was interested in a large tell with fairly continuous
occupation in the Bronze and Iron ages and as little later debris
as possible. The group wanted a site with biblical connections,
one offering possibilities of epigraphic finds, one with potentialities for several campaigns, and one which could be excavated
during the summer. The last requirement eliminated sites in the
Jordan valley, and there was one tell which held out far more
promise than any other, Ta'annek.[7] In fact, after Ta'annek the
next most promising sites were in Syria.

Many of the minor excavations in Palestine have been prompted
by chance discoveries, some by a scholarly concern with a particular

problem; others are salvage operations. The clearance of the
Wâdî ed-Dâliyeh caves was prompted by the discovery of the
Samaria Papyri there.[8] (This find, incidentally, provides some
justification for the Jordan government's closed-eye policy on
some of the illegal digging for antiquities by bedouin. These
documents would certainly never have been discovered by an
archaeologist!) The excavation at 'Arâq el-Emîr was undertaken
primarily to secure stratified remains of the fifth and fourth
centuries B.C.[9] A sounding was undertaken at Tell er-Rumeith
to gather evidence on its identification with Ramoth-gilead and
to see if it offered promise for a large excavation (Pl. 29).[10]
One of the aims of the Jerusalem excavation is to "salvage" the
remains from open areas of Jerusalem which are about to be covered
with modern structures, and a dig is proposed for Gibeah (Tell
el-Fûl) next spring to glean information from its antiquities
before the proposed palace for King Hussein is built there.[11]

What all this suggests is that it is quite unlikely under
present circumstances that any imposed program of excavation could
improve upon the present flexible situation, in which expeditions
are free to select sites in terms of their interests and qualifications while at the same time competent groups are available to
handle urgent archaeological projects. With such vast amounts
of material to be dug and such immense gaps in our knowledge,
any competent person willing to devote time toward filling in
the gaps should be welcomed and encouraged by all interested in
Palestine's past.

The factors discussed above are important elements in the
perspective with which any reader should want to approach reports
on archaeological work in Palestine. Interpretations and conclusions about excavated material are commonly based on a tiny
fraction of the potential evidence, and the representative character of this is often impossible to determine. As archaeological
methodology is refined and digging tends to become more and more
meticulous, the extent of an excavation will tend to decrease in
proportion to the size of the staff and amount of technical equipment required. As a result the body of material on Palestine will
probably not grow at a much faster pace in the near future than
it is at present. Palestine will remain mostly unknown for many
years to come unless some modern device such as the magnetometer
is perfected to the point that a clear picture of the contents of
a mound can be secured without the tedious processes of excavation.

Interpreting and Reporting

In view of the above discussion, specifying limitations in
archaeological reporting is especially crucial. In the social and
physical sciences, comparable human or laboratory circumstances

may be repeated to test a given hypothesis, but an archaeologist cannot easily make another slice through his mound to test his hypothesis about, let us say, an unusual Late Bronze building. An ideal final archaeological report should make it possible for the reader to reconstruct the layers and associated structures and artifacts as they existed before excavation, but up to now this goal has not been approached even by the best archaeological publications. No one is in as advantageous a position as the archaeologist himself to understand the limitations of his evidence, and it is crucial that he report them.

The treatment of the Sacred Area in the preliminary report of the latest campaign at Shechem (a model of prompt and detailed reporting) may prove instructive at this point.[12] The chief hypothesis is that the structure under the Fortress Temple forecourt, previously designated a palace, is now to be interpreted as a courtyard temple like Temples I and II at Bogazköy. From a table summarizing the history of the Sacred Area the conclusion might be drawn that the sacred character of the courtyard phase is as assured as that of the Fortress Temple. Such a conclusion would seem dubious, since the Fortress Temple lies completely exposed for all to see while important parts of the courtyard phase, not specified clearly on the plans, remain unexcavated. As is common in a preliminary report, the hypothesis seems to be set forth in the most favorable light. The Bogazköy parallels are considered remarkable, but differences such as the separation of the chief cult room from the central court are not specified. Possible objections to the hypothesis such as the lack of cult objects and installations, the occurrence of domestic jar burials and ovens in the temple, and the presence of a noncultic structure within the sacred temenos are not considered.

The archaeologist is constantly tempted or forced to expand theories upon a small evidential base. He builds his hypotheses on the small excavated portion of a building complex or installation or on tatters of buildings disturbed by later occupation. He frequently uses arguments from silence based upon the absence of certain phenomena or artifacts when he has excavated only a tiny fraction of a mound or merely from surface finds. He has to describe nearly all structures without benefit of literary evidence or epigraphic finds. Sometimes whole building complexes leave little hint of their function.

There comes to mind immediately the well-known story of the archaeologist who related evidence of a large silt layer covering the area he was excavating to the great flood only to discover later on that the "great flood" had destroyed only a small part of his mound. Even more distressing is the way in which his original announcement of finding the flood has been perpetuated in the popular volumes which report archaeological finds to the

public. In digging a Middle Bronze I cemetery this past month
the first week was occupied with clearing some ten tombs in
cemeteries with evidence of some 85 tombs visible from surface
exploration. On the basis of this comparatively large sample
we could have concluded that all the tombs were either robbed
or their contents covered with heavy roof fall, but, happily,
results of the second week belied that conclusion.[13]

The shaded portion of the general plan of the Taanach excavations (Pl. 19) illustrates what a small part of that tell was
investigated in the 1963 campaign with a comparatively large
staff and labor force, and only a small part of the shaded areas
was actually excavated at bedrock. The other excavated areas
shown on the plan are the work of three campaigns carried out by
the German scholar E. Sellin in 1902-1904. With the less rigorous
methods of digging in vogue at the beginning of this century nearly
a fifth of the mound was excavated. Even these extensive operations
did not provide sufficient evidence for Sellin's conclusions that
there were no more important structures to be found on the site and
that the city had never been surrounded by a fortification wall,
for both were found in this season's excavation.

The wall fragments in the "Cult Area" of the Taanach plan
point up the problem of interpretation involved when only portions
of buildings are preserved. The excavator would like to be able
to propose a reconstruction for the building and indicate how the
inhabitants under Jeroboam I (922-901 B.C.) were using the building
before it was violently destroyed in the late tenth century, possibly
by Pharaoh Shishak in 918 B.C. Important for the interpretation
are the finds from the destruction layer inside the building (Pl. 20).
They include objects of a cultic nature such as over a hundred pig
ankle bones and an Astarte figurine mold, as well as noncultic
objects including many large jars, some containing grain, over fifty
large loom weights, about a dozen iron weapons and implements, and
several weights. A detailed study of comparable material has not
yet been made, but any attempt to complete the lines of the wall
fragments along lines of what might be a similar cult structure
should be undertaken with extreme caution. In fact, to be at all
convincing the attribution of the function of the building will
have to account for the noncultic as well as the cultic artifacts.
It has been suggested that these remains provide background for the
cultic and commercial activities of an enterprising group of priests
who combined the sale of grain and loom weights with that of
amulets and figurines, but this merely represents one of several
possibilities. Perhaps this was the residence of the local medium
or witch and perhaps the materials were not for sale at all but
part of a sanctuary store.

The Late Bronze I complex at Taanach is a well-preserved series
of rooms covering a fairly large area. It illustrates the problem

of interpretation facing the archaeologist even when his evidence is left fairly undisturbed by later occupation. The complex so far excavated consisted of six rooms and an open court with a tramped earth floor. Five of the rooms had plastered floors and the floor of the sixth consisted of two large slabs of soft limestone. Two of the rooms were only four by four feet. Besides the usual masses of sherds, only a few nearly intact bowls and juglets, a broken water pipe, three fragments of a new type of plaque Astarte figurine, and a curious stone-lined circular pit plastered with a red clayey mortar were left by the ancient inhabitants to offer clues as to the function of the building. Even considering the poverty of comparative material from fifteenth century B.C. Palestine, the preliminary conclusion that this complex served "some industrial or storage purpose" is far from satisfying.

There is another aspect in the background of archaeological reporting which is too delicate to attempt to illustrate but is nevertheless an important factor for the reader of archaeological accounts to consider. It involves the pressures which commonly face archaeologists when they write their reports—pressures toward glossing over the limitations of the evidence and the weak points in hypotheses and toward inflating the importance of finds and maximizing interpretations. With a disappointing campaign the morale of the expedition staff might disintegrate; patrons might be less inclined to future generosity; colleagues might accord the expedition reduced prestige. When space is limited, what archaeologist, having reached bedrock at the end of an exhausting campaign, would not stress the exciting finds thirty feet down rather than that only three square yards of bedrock were uncovered? Pressed for an immediate report or news release at the end of a dig, it is difficult for an archaeologist to avoid piecing together creditable hypotheses, unsubstantiated interpretations, and experienced guesses into a "story" in which the reader frequently is at pains to distinguish a substantial hypothesis from a guess. An archaeologist would be as foolish to deny that such pressures exist as to claim that such pressures have had no influence on his reporting.

While we must content ourselves with interpretations of archaeological material which are for the most part far from satisfying, the flood of new evidence, bringing with it new and developing hypotheses and emerging pictures of ancient Palestine, makes Palestinian archaeology an attractive and challenging discipline for archaeologists and biblical scholars alike. Another writer on the scene dealing with the archaeological potential of Palestine would have used other illustrations, but the dominating impression could hardly be changed: Palestinian archaeology is in its childhood with a wide open, promising future.

Chapter V

THE EXCAVATIONS AT 'ARÂQ EL-EMÎR

Three campaigns were undertaken at 'Arâq el-Emîr in 1961
and 1962. The budget was supplied principally by the American
Schools of Oriental Research along with substantial grants from
the Iliff School of Theology in 1961 and Princeton University in
1962. Most of the staff members were appointees and residents of
the Jerusalem School, many of these gaining their first archaeological field experience. The Department of Antiquities of Jordan
facilitated the work by taking ownership of part of the village
land and by supplying a railroad. The three campaigns involved
some fifteen weeks of excavation with a work force varying from
50 to 130 workers and staffs of from eight to sixteen.

The third campaign took place between September 10 and
October 12, 1962.[1] Except for a minor operation outside one of
the caves, work was concentrated exclusively at the Qasr and in
the northwest quarter of the village where the work of the
earlier campaigns was continued (Pl. 2). The most striking find
of the campaign was a feline sculptured in high relief on a block
of mottled red and white dolomite (Pl. 3). It came to light as
debris was being cleared from the face of the Qasr east wall near
its north end. According to its Hellenistic plan, the Qasr was
to be surrounded by a large lake, the extent of which can be
appreciated by observing the depressed area which still surrounds
the Qasr. A road skirted the south embankment of the lake and
passed northward through Gate II and Gate I (Pl. 2). From Gate I
the main path continued north to the village and caves, but just
inside the gate a path led westward across the only spur of land
through the lake to the Qasr. The feline sculpture was on a line
with this path, greeting all visitors as they approached.

The feline functioned as a fountain. Inside the Qasr were
traces of a plastered basin with a channel leading to the animal's
mouth. In the sculptured megalith the conduit consisted of a
narrow circular hole which widened to a 5 by 7 cm. rectangular
opening in the feline's mouth without teeth or tongue. That a
pool to receive the water stream from the mouth must have been
planned is indicated by a channel just in front of the animal's
right forepaw (Pl. 3). Whether such a pool had ever been completed could not be determined, for Byzantine occupation layers
occur to a considerable depth below the fountain megalith, which
rests on the upper surface of the Hellenistic Qasr foundations.
A Byzantine wall, set against the outer face of the Qasr east wall
and carefully built around the sculptured block, has certainly
contributed to its fine state of preservation and its concealment
before our excavations.

The maximum dimensions of the sculptured block are 2.05 by
1.50 meters. It is 35 cm. thick and in addition the relief
projects as much as 45 cm. A stone cut around the animal's head
caps the sculptured stone and levels with the 1.75 m. height of
the lowest course into which the block is set. Smaller undressed
stones were used to fill out the 90 cm. width of the megalithic
course inside (Pl. 4). The 2.05 m. length is unique for megaliths
of the lowest course of the east wall so that the placement of the
fountain seems to have been part of the original building plan.
Its crude insertion suggests that it was probably placed after the
wall had been erected.

The possibility that the relief had been used in another
setting or was available when the Qasr architects made their plans
cannot be excluded. It will be noted below that the carving of
the animal frieze was completed in situ. It could be argued that
the same procedure would be expected with the fountain relief had
it not been already prepared. The writer would prefer the view
that the relief was commissioned in connection with the building
of the Qasr and inserted after the hazards from erecting megalithic
walls had passed. The relief block was of mottled red and white
dolomite breccia, which is locally available. From the view point
of the history of art there is nothing against its execution in
the early second century B.C., when the Qasr was built (see below).
Excavation so far has not brought to light any evidence of monumental buildings in the area of the third century B.C., and the
large-scale building operations of Hyrcanus display enough evidence
of planning to make it difficult to consider the animal fountain
as originally planned for any other place than where it was found.

It seems doubtful that the sculptor had a specific beast in
mind for the relief. The male body seems too sleek for a lion,
not sleek enough for a leopard or panther. The head, too, seems
small for a lion, large for a leopard. The tail tuft belongs to
a lion, but the curling of the tail around one leg is a more common
treatment for leopards. The griffin-like claws occur on Greek
monumental lions, but the mane, which is a characteristic feature
of the male lion, is missing. The mottled stone gives the beast
a spotted appearance, which is the monument's most striking feature.
Dr. Dorothy Hill suggests that the feline is a result of the combination of the sculptor's (distant?) knowledge of sculptured lions,
sphinxes, and griffins, and his acquaintance with live Transjor-
danian leopards.

In attempting to assess the artistic tradition which produced
this work of art, Miss Hill points out "that there is no other
known monument like the animal fountain of 'Arâq el-Emîr." Indeed,
we have very little evidence at all of the effective influences
upon works of art in Syria-Palestine and of the entire Near East
in the second century B.C. Whole lions or leopards as fountains

were rare in the Greek world though the heads of lions were
commonly used as spouts. Lion spouts seem to be unknown outside
the Greek world. The unequal lengths of the legs is a Greek
means of portraying action. The animal with extended paw is a
common Greek stance of the Hellenistic period, though only one of
the expected antithetical pair appears here. These and other
observations have led Miss Hill to define the fountain as "a
provincial Greek work of the period 182-175 B.C."[2]

A second major discovery of the third campaign was conclusive
evidence that the Qasr was never completed. Evidence that the Qasr
was unfinished had been available to Butler when he published his
detailed study of the Qasr early in this century, but he did not
find it convincing. In connection with getting evidence for Mr.
Michael Brett's restored plan of the Qasr, an attempt was made to
jack up all megaliths of the frieze course; they could easily be
picked out by their dimensions. In raising one of them near the
southwest corner of the building, it was surprising to find that
the lion had only been roughed out for carving. Since the block
had obviously fallen from the building, it was to have been finished
in situ.

Shortly after this discovery several other unfinished elements
were noted. The dentils of the string course of the north porch
had not been cut in a fragment from the east corner, whereas they
had been cut in the adjacent fragment of this course. The carefully dressed west semicolumn of the north porch was set against
a megalith only roughly finished on the inside. A quite unexpected
discovery came to light as the lowest dressed course of the east
Qasr wall was being uncovered. One of the megaliths had a smooth
surface, its boss having been completely removed. The boss of an
adjacent megalith was obviously in the process of being removed
when work on the building ceased. The observation that the margins
and bosses throughout the Qasr are quite irregular suggests that
the completed building would have had a smooth face.

To these discoveries should be added some of the evidence
previously cited for the unfinished state of the building. A
base for one of the north porch free-standing columns had a projecting ring, which had presumably been used in transport of the
block but was not subsequently removed. Some of the Corinthian
style capitals show remarkably detailed finish, but in others the
details have only been roughed out. Other non-Hellenistic capitals
have been only roughly blocked out. Together this evidence points
to the fact that the outer shell of the Qasr had been erected, but
much detailed finishing was left undone. The problem of the extent
to which the inside of the building was completed is more difficult.
It is connected with the problem of the function of the building,
to which we now turn.

After the 1961 campaigns an attempt was made to develop the
hypothesis that the Qasr was a mausoleum, the view of Albright.[3]

Mr. Brett's architectural study of the Qasr has drawn attention to
the stairwell east of the north porch (Pl. 4).[4] The flights of
wide, low steps gave access to a gallery and led to a tower above
the frieze course. Presumably they were also to have given access
to a terrace roof. Although there is no evidence that the roof
had been completed, the megalithic foundation lines (Pl. 4) are
best interpreted as lines of support for a roof. Among the
Byzantine walls and occupation debris (which lay well below the
level of the Hellenistic floor) there was no clear evidence of a
terrace roof, and certainly if it had been completed, some
vestiges would have survived. Just what had been completed inside
at the time of Hyrcanus and what might have been reused by the
Byzantine occupants is impossible to decide.

In any case, Robert Amy has convincingly shown that these
elements--stairway, tower, and terrace roof--are present in some
39 temples and are to be associated with a cult function.[5] Other
features of the Qasr find their best parallels in temples. The
bifaciality of the Qasr (which leaves a nonfunctional south porch)
has parallels in temples from Syria to Sicily. Megalithic voussoir
blocks have been found at the Qasr only in the vicinity of the
adytum of the temple. Other temples are associated with bodies of
water. Perhaps the chief reason for hesitating to call the building a temple has been the view that such a rival to the Jerusalem
temple was impossible. Such a view ignores Josephus' reference
to the nearly contemporary temple at Leontopolis in Egypt. Certainly, the religious significance of the Qasr will be an important
subject of study for years to come.

In the first two campaigns evidence for dating the Qasr was
extremely elusive. Byzantine occupation had cut down to the Early
Bronze layers upon which the Qasr was built. Despite the lack of
stratigraphic evidence, there was no hesitation about considering
the building, as described by Josephus, Hellenistic. Yet, some
scholars preferred a date a century earlier than that indicated in
Josephus' account. This matter was settled by the discovery in the
1962 campaign of a satisfactory group of Hellenistic potsherds
clearly belonging to the first half of the second century B.C. The
complete lack of anything from the third century B.C., at the Qasr
or the Square Building[6] makes any attempt to raise the date of the
building unjustified. The evidence that the Qasr was unfinished
makes the seven-year period (ca. 182-175 B.C.) in which Josephus
has Hyrcanus at 'Arâq el-Emîr less difficult for the major operations accomplished, but it is not impossible that Hyrcanus began
his operations as early as 210 B.C., and his death could have
occurred a few years after 175 B.C.

Of the Byzantine occupation of the Qasr little new was learned
in the third campaign. The general chronological framework proposed
after the first campaign received additional support.

The highlight of the 1962 excavation in the village was the discovery of the Plaster Building. Excavation was extended west from the west wall of the Late Hellenistic town with the aim of learning more about the heavy Iron I walls previously excavated. This purpose was completely frustrated by Hellenistic builders, who had cleared away Iron age remains for their construction. As so far excavated (Pl. 5), the building consists of an area of over 18 by 21 m. surrounded by a wall of medium and small stones some 90 cm. thick, with two thin coats of white plaster on its inner face. A second wall, placed concentrically inside this area, contains an area of some 10.5 by 15 m. This wall is 1.15 m. thick and is plastered on its outer face like the outside wall, but on its inner face with a much thicker beautiful dark red plaster with bevelled edges and white borders. The base of this wall at the doorways is composed of finely dressed rectangular blocks, but the rest of the wall consists of plaster against dirt and rubble. There was a single entrance to the inner court in the middle of the east wall, two symmetrically placed doorways in the inner south wall, one at the west end of the inner north wall, and presumably others still unexcavated. All these were about 1.10 m. wide. Between the two walls was a corridor 2.70 m. wide with an extremely hard-packed floor, and the inner court had a similar, but less well-made floor. Except for a drain at the outer wall near the northwest corner and some mysterious paving blocks interrupting the northwest entryway, there was no evidence of any kind unearthed to shed light on the function of the building.

The ashy layer which covered the floor of the corridor and part of the inner court contained a pottery group which belongs about 175 B.C. A very small sounding below the floor yielded sherds which are probably to be assigned to the early second century B.C. To the west, where the walls of the building were only preserved as foundations, we obtained our first good group of Hellenistic sherds which can be assigned with confidence to the very beginning of the second century B.C. This evidence points strongly to the construction of the Plaster Building at the time of Hyrcanus who "built enclosures [aulai] remarkable for their size, and adorned them with vast parks."[7] It is difficult to dissociate the Plaster Building from the aulai, for by one definition an aule is a court or quadrangle "round which the house itself was built, having a corridor all around".

The basic stratigraphy in the village, described in earlier reports, has proved essentially correct, but some refinements should be noted. Strata I (ca. A.D. 200) and II (ca. A.D. 100) remain the same. Strata IIIa (ca. A.D. 50) and IIIb (ca. 100 B.C.) are unchanged, but Stratum IV becomes an earlier Hellenistic phase (ca. 175 B.C.). Stratum IV of the first campaign becomes the Iron I Stratum V (ca. 1050 B.C.). Early Bronze surfaces appearing in a limited area are designated as Stratum VI.

The change in strata designation became necessary when detailed study after the third campaign made it clear that the original Stratum IIIb consisted of two elements. Stratum IIIb consisted of the northern and western town walls with inner walls parallel to these joined by crosswalls forming a casemate-type construction. A wall at the southern end of the excavated area bounded a large courtyard inside the casemates. Most of the Stratum IIIb walls were laid on a plaster floor of high quality some 5 cm. thick, while the plaster floor of the court was of poorer quality. Elsewhere foundations for Stratum IIIb walls cut through the thick plaster floor, and the trench was covered by plaster of poorer quality so that the line of the joining of the two qualities of plaster could be noted. The evidence led to a careful rechecking of material below the better and poorer quality plaster in the casemates, and it became clear that the few pockets of Early Hellenistic pottery recovered in the excavation were sealed under the thicker plaster floor.

This evidence forced the conclusion that the plaster floor unearthed over so much of the excavated area had been used during two phases of occupation. The thicker plaster floor was assigned to Stratum IV, for it became clear that it had extended beyond the IIIb north and west village walls and must have been part of a large building of which only a few vestiges remains. These included drainage channels cut into bedrock, two curious stone pavings several protrusions of bedrock unintelligible in their IIIb setting, and a column base plastered into the thick plaster floor. In only one of the casemate rooms were discovered separate IIIb and IV floors, and here the remnant of Stratum IV walls were covered with beautiful painted plaster, similar to that of the Plaster Building. This combined with other evidence suggests that the large plaster-floor structure of Stratum IV and the Plaster Building are contemporary, both the work of Hyrcanus.

This isolation of Hellenistic Stratum IV provides an explanation for the lack so far of Persian and Early Hellenistic remains in the excavations though we have been shown artifacts of this time which certainly come from the village. The laying of the Stratum IV floor involved cutting down several bedrock outcroppings and the scraping away of all earlier occupation debris to below the level of the Stratum V floors. The few pockets of Early Hellenistic sherds below the Stratum IV floors may be considered the bottoms of Hellenistic pits which had been cut into the Iron age layers.

The Strata IIIa, II, and I occupations continued to have the same character as in previous campaigns, and their dates remain the same. The progressive additions of crosswalls in the casemates and large court in Strata II and I was studied in detail, and their progressively poorer quality was noted. This reflects the change

of the area from a public function to domestic dwellings, which
tended to become more crowded, presumably as the population of
the town increased. We were fortunate enough to recover quite
a number of new forms for the ceramic groups of Strata II and I,
including quite a number of whole or reconstructed pieces.

It seems likely that ʿArâq el-Emîr is to be identified with
Ramath-mizpeh of the Old Testament, and Birta ("stronghold") of
the Ammanitis in the Land of Tobiah mentioned in the Zenon papyri.
It is certainly the Tyros built by Hyrcanus in the early second
century B.C. Of the sites proposed for Ramath-mizpeh (Khirbet
Jelʿâd, Khirbet es-Sâr, Khirbet es-Sîreh), only ʿArâq el-Emîr
has both a geographically satisfactory position and evidence of
Iron I occupation.

Chapter VI

THE CAVE CLEARANCES OF THE WĀDĪ ED-DĀLIYEH

Jerusalem - February 1, 1963[1]

Late one afternoon last April Père R. de Vaux of the École
Biblique and Mr. Yusef Saad, Curator of the Palestine Archaeological Museum, paid a visit to the School. They were excited about
the contents of a tiny box they brought with them. In it was a
small piece of worm-eaten papyrus with Aramaic written on both
sides. We spent most of the night consulting our palaeography
notes and charts and combing Aramaic dictionaries. The next
morning we reported to Père de Vaux that the script belonged
about 375 B.C., that the fragment was part of an official document probably having to do with military administration, and that,
although the fragment was too small to make continuous sense, the
city of Samaria was clearly mentioned. So began the story of the
Samaria Papyri.

The papyrus sample was part of a larger find consisting of
many more fragments, some small rolls of papyrus (one still sealed
with seven sealings), a collection of several dozen sealings
(bearing distinct Persian and Greek figures), and a few coins--all
reportedly from a cave some distance north of Jericho. These were
purportedly discovered by diggers of the Ta'âmireh tribe in late
March or early April. Attempts on all sides to raise funds and
negotiate a reasonable purchase price went on through October.

When we returned from the fall trip on 3 November we learned
about a fund established within the ASOR, which would provide
funds for purchasing publishing rights of manuscripts such as the
Samaria Papyri. Professor Frank M. Cross, Jr., was appointed
chairman of a committee to administer the fund, and he flew out
to Jerusalem arriving 14 November to negotiate for the papyri.

By 19 November negotiations were complete, and Professor
Cross could begin studying the documents. The agreement enabled
the Palestine Archaeological Museum to purchase the papyri with
exclusive rights of publication reserved for Professor Cross
representing ASOR. That first night Nancy and I watched with
baited breath while Professor Cross' deft hand cut the seven
seals of the "prize piece". The fragile papyrus became pliable
again when water was applied with a fine brush and the unrolling
began. The flattened roll was unwound six turns and still no
writing appeared! The next turn revealed that the original document was wider, had had several more sealings, and on the missing
portion signatures could be expected at the bottom where our piece
was blank. When the top line was reached, Professor Cross

immediately read: The twentieth day of Adar, year two, the accession year of the reign of Darius. The reference was to the second year of Arsemes and the first of Darius III, 335 B.C. With the subsequent discovery that one of the coins was minted by Mazdai in the last years of Darius III, came strong support for an hypothesis about the materials developed by Professor Cross: The documents were taken to the cave by refugees fleeing from Samaria when Alexander's forces destroyed it in 331 B.C.

After Professor Cross' departure on 25 November, our interest was concentrated on locating the cave from which the manuscripts came. On 2 December a Ta'âmireh guide led Mr. Saad to the site. He brought back some Iron II (eighth century B.C.) sherds and a report of the long, difficult, and adventuresome walk to the cave from a point about a kilometer west of Khirbet Fasayil. Having gone in the afternoon, he did not have time to explore the cave interior but hurried back to reach his car before nightfall.

Mr. Saad engaged a Ta'âmireh guide to lead Père de Vaux, Nancy and me to the cave on 11 December. When the Ta'âmireh failed to appear, we left for Fasayil with Mr. Saad as our guide. Driving west over the trackless waste west of Fasayil we were unable to locate any Ta'âmireh tribesmen. The few shepherd boys in the neighborhood ran off when we called them. Finally, one man appeared to greet us, but he persisted in his ignorance about the cave until Mr. Saad was able to assure him we were not spies. He then led us on an hour-and-a-half walk to the cave area (Pl. 6). It was honeycombed with caves, and in most of them heaps of sifted earth testified to the industry of the Ta'âmireh diggers. The first cave we examined had a large mouth with a tiny passage about large enough for a slender Ta'âmireh to squirm through at the back. Here we collected MB I (20th century B.C.) and Early Roman sherds.

The caves are situated on either side of a narrow gorge of the Wâdī ed-Dâliyeh. A cascade divides the caves into an upper (western) and a lower (eastern) group. The caves just mentioned were in the upper group, but Mr. Saad called us to the lower group where he had located the manuscript cave. While we ate our lunch at the entrance we noticed pieces of human skulls and picked up Early Bronze, Iron II, and Early Roman pottery. After lunch we prepared our lamps and crawled on all fours from the mouth to the interior of the cave (Pl. 7). It extended into the cliffs as far as our lamps could reach, some 65 meters as we later measured. Walking, crawling, bobbling our heads to avoid bats and overhanging rocks and covering our faces to avoid as much of the guano dust as we could, we reached the far end of the cave, the place later confirmed as the manuscript find spot. Noting the vast amount of sifted debris and picking up the first pottery that was clearly fourth century B.C., we took another passage and climbed a rather steep ascent to the "bat dome" (Pl. 8). This was a large

cavernous room with several longer passages leading from it. Its
ceiling was covered with literally layers of screeching bats. We
followed one of its passages some 20 meters and found here the
same human bones and early Hellenistic pottery that we saw at the
manuscript find spot and the passage leading to it. By then we
were all ready for some fresh air and the walk back to Fasayil.

Our discussions of plans for sounding in the caves became less
and less excited and more and more sober as we trudged back to the
Land-Rover. Logistics would be the chief problem. How could we
get camping gear to the site over paths impossible for donkeys?
What arrangements could be made to supply the site with water from
five miles away? Could we get workers when the drought was driving
the Ta'âmireh considerably north of Fasayil? Where could a camp
be placed when there was no flat land nearby? What kinds of masks
and goggles could be obtained immediately for work in the dust, and
what kind of lighting would be satisfactory for the caves? Would
the bats present problems? Just what could be done with the small
amount left in our archaeology budget? Then, too, the visit indicated that prospects for results were only fair. The pottery would
probably be mixed. The large amounts of sterile debris sifted by
the Ta'âmireh would take much time to sift through with prospects
for perhaps nothing more than a few tiny pieces of papyrus--if we
were lucky. There were some places that seemed untouched by
digging, and, in any case, the job had to be done.

Deciding to postpone work until after Christmas, we set 7
January as the first day of digging and decided to dig two--and if
circumstances demanded it three--weeks. I took a foreman, technical
man, a first load of gear, and driver to the site on 4 January to
see if the logistics problems could be surmounted. Enough progress
was made to justify a firm decision to go ahead. We decided that
we would have to pitch some of our tents in the mouths of caves on
both sides of the wadi and others were to be nestled against the
bases of the sheer cliffs of the wadi after terraces were constructed (Pl. 6). (Those of us living within shadows of the cliffs
tried to forget what might happen if rock above became dislodged
or if it rained.) Faithful Ali agreed--for a price--to supply us
with water by a circuitous path his donkeys could negotiate, and
he persuaded about ten of his friends to stay on and work--for a
price. In any case, no wage seemed unreasonable for climbing wadis
five miles each way to work and working seven hours and a half in
choking dust each day.

At a farewell for departing Honorary Associates Dorothy Hill,
George Landes, and Fellow Jack Holladay the details of the find and
proposed soundings were told to our residents with the help of Père
de Vaux, and almost immediately the staff became clear. Fellow Alex
Di Lella, O.F.M., was immediately eager to participate as was W. F.
Albright Fellow Willis Shotwell when he arrived a few days later.
Miss Hill postponed her departure and became a third field supervisor,

and Dr. Awni Dajani, Director of the Jordan Department of
Antiquities, sent along Miss Najua Husseini as Department
Representative--and an excellent field supervisor. Mr. Michael
Brett, architect for 'Arâq el-Emîr, spent the first week with us
getting the plan of the manuscript cave. Back in Jerusalem Annual
Professor R. B. Y. Scott served as object recorder and Mrs. Nancy
Lapp as pottery recorder. The Department of Antiquities answered
our need for an additional supervisor for the second week by
sending Mr. Sami Rashid, but, unfortunately, he had trouble with
his teeth and had to return before the end of the week. Muhammed
Adawi served as our very capable cook, and Abed Dhib Nsif (Aboud),
newly hired as a driver-gardner for the School on a temporary
basis, served as driver and assisted in dig supervision. Nasir
Diab from Balâtah rendered outstanding service as a technical
man. Most equipment needed was on hand at the School, but sister
institutions were most cooperative in filling in the gaps. Père
de Vaux of the École Biblique and Mr. Sami Maddah of the Department
of Antiquities let us borrow masks which were most helpful to our
staff, and Mrs. Crystal Bennett of the British School loaned us
flood lamps.

Friday night, when the foreman we were counting on to begin
setting up camp the next day refused to work without a raise in
pay, Fellows Di Lella and Shotwell rallied to the occasion,
accompanied our second load of gear out Saturday morning, helped
see that the donkeys packed it to the cave area safely, and began
setting up camp with the aid of Nasir Diab and six Ta'âmireh.
Aboud took Muhammed and our food out Sunday morning and the rest
of us after Sunday dinner at the School. Our worries about logistics problems were dissolved by the hard work of the camp crew.
When we arrived at dusk the picturesque camp nestled in the wadi
was 100% ready for living and work! Soon the supper bell rang, and
after our usual first dig meal (corned beef, cheese, and peanut
butter sandwiches) and some discussion of dig procedures, we retired
early, excited at the prospects of what tomorrow would bring.

By shortly after 7 a.m. we were delighted to find that 14
Ta'âmireh had appeared for work. Our plan was to start one crew
working in the purported manuscript find area lead by the careful
digging of Nasir Diab, divide the remaining workers into two crews
which would begin a trench from the mouth of the cave to the manuscript area (Pl. 8). This trench would serve three purposes: it
would make it possible to reach the inside of the cave without the
tiring crawl and squirm; it would reveal any openings or passages
in the rock that might have been missed by the treasure-hunters on
one side or the other of the passage; and, most important, it
would provide a key to the history of the cave's occupation. We
were amazed that by the end of the day the two crews had already
extended the trench inward some 15 meters from the mouth of the

cave--the trench already being over a meter deep in spots.
(Perhaps we should have expected hard work, for in the time
between our December visit and the beginning of the work a
tremendous amount of dirt had been sifted in the cave.) Mean-
while the manuscript area was producing 14 full baskets of
pottery (nearly all our 331 B.C. horizon), human bones and
skulls, cloth and sticks.

By the second day we were up to 26 workers and sent a fourth
crew up to work in the cave with the squirm hole (in the mouth of
which we had put our kitchen tent). Father Di Lella was put in
charge of Cave II where there was more air and less dust.
Immediately Early Roman and Middle Bronze I potsherds began to
show up in abundance. In Cave I the trenching operations indicated that a rather large alcove had not been touched by previous
digging, and a trench into it indicated the stratigraphy of the
same occupational history as the manuscript area: fourth century
B.C. pots and bones covered by a thin scattering of Early Roman
sherds. The manuscript area still gave no clear indication we
were in the right spot, but the first evidence of food not consumed turned up in the form of date skins.

On 9 January, our third day of digging, came the first
papyrus fragments which confirmed the find spot of the manuscripts.
By now the number of skulls from that spot had increased to about
35, including men, women, and children of all ages and large
quantities of cloth (some beautifully embroidered), wood, olive
and date pits, sycamine nuts. We were especially interested in
mat fragments in connection with the story told by Ta'âmireh who
were among the first to enter the cave. They reported some 300
skeletons lying on mats in the cave. The best hypothesis to
explain this (and subsequent) evidence seemed to be: Alexander's
troops found this hiding place of the leading refugees from
Samaria and suffocated them by building a large fire at the mouth
of the cave. In any case, evidence clearly pointed to a catastrophe in which a large number of refugees from Samaria perished in
a cave simultaneously.

The surprise of our fourth day came when the trench in Cave II
reached the inner room. Not only was this a large room, it led to
another 1500 feet of passages into the rock with many side passages--
mostly unexplored by Ta'âmireh. At Cave I the trench was nearing
completion, much of it dug in undisturbed debris, and many more
baskets of pots, bones, and other materials already mentioned (including papyri) continued to come from the manuscript area.

By Friday we were all ready for a rest, but our largest piece
of papyrus with six aramaic letters and a deep, four-spouted MB I
lamp from Cave II buoyed up our spirits. The trench was completed,
and it was now easy to get to the manuscript area. We paid the
workers, hired two watchmen, and left for the weekend.

Our work was handicapped by a lack of good lighting, and Aboud and I spent Saturday in Jerusalem and Amman trying to locate a small generator that could be transported to the site and some batteries for flood lights. We could find neither, so we increased the number of our wick lanterns and had to continue working with them. In Cave II pressure lamps could be used, but in Cave I they consumed too much oxygen and produced too much heat. Dr. Dajani was very encouraging and helpful when we visited his office, and I helped him prepare a brief release on our findings.

After an uneventful trip back in and a good night's sleep (no barking dogs), we were prepared for a rather uneventful week, but exciting finds continued. In fact, Monday was probably our most exciting day. First, came the visit of a group of villagers from Mughayir, the nearest village to the west of the caves. Here at last were people who could tell us where we were on our maps. The manuscript cave was Mugharet Abu Shinjeh, and Cave II was one of the 'Arâq en-Na'sâneh. They had with them a beautiful Middle Bronze tomb group from a cave opened recently near their village, and they promised to shut off the cave until we would pay them to continue digging it. Being the owners of the land around the caves, they hoped to be hired for any future work at the caves. I could hardly wait to leave the villagers to see the surprise Father Di Lella had waiting for me in Cave II--three large MB I jars, each of a different type and nearly complete. One had combed design on its shoulder and still contained grain, and the others were decorated with various rope and thumb-impressed moldings. Four more jars of similar types came to light during the week with large pieces of smaller vessels--carinated bowls and burnished jugs and juglets (Pl. 10). The exciting finds of the day in the Cave I manuscript area were one of the clay sealings like those purchased with the papyri and a beautiful small scarab which Père Couroyer is provisionally content to assign to a fourth or third century B.C. artisan in Palestine. We assigned one of our crews to a passage off the "bat dome," and while there were no surprises, the same pots and dolichocephalic skulls continued to appear. The day was topped by an accurate account of the dig on the evening news broadcast of the Hashemite Broadcasting Service.

The next day digging brought no new excitement, but after work a Mughayir villager led us to the Mugharet ed-Dâliyeh, which he claimed was larger than either of the caverns we were excavating. He pointed out evidence that Ta'âmireh were just beginning to work the cave, but the passages to the interior were blocked and we did not explore further. We also explored Mugharet Shi'b el-Qubûr slightly to the north and considered both caves worthy of at least a small sounding.

Wednesday we had a group of 12 visitors: Dr. Dajani and three members of the Department of Antiquities, a group from the École Biblique led by Père de Vaux, Mrs. Crystal Bennett from the British

School, Miss Diana Kirkbride, Father William Casey, and Mrs. Nancy Lapp. We were able to use the new trench to take the group through the cave with relative ease, and we surprised the group with the large pots in the upper cave, which we had left in situ "for show".

Besides the find of a beautiful silver earring in the manuscript area (Ta'âmireh reported a gold ring and golden earrings had also been found), the sounding ended quietly with no necessity to consider a third week--the entire job would take much longer. We were quite excited that the three large MB I pots that started from the dig nearly whole reached the School in the same condition late Saturday evening, having been carried out to the Land-Rover by Ta'âmireh by hand. That night we could finally relax again thankful that such a dangerous operation had been completed with no major mishaps--and with a wealth of important material for study. We need to contact specialists to study the importance of the cloth for the history of textiles; an anthropologist to analyze the importance of the skeletons of the Samaritans, an object of special study in that field; someone to analyze the kinds of wood found with the manuscript fragments; and a detailed study of the homogeneous ceramic group from the beginning of the Hellenistic era, a study on which my wife is already making progress.

A word must be said about the unbelievable Ta'âmireh who worked for us. Their strength was amazing. They worked at least twice as hard as any workmen I've ever seen on any previous dig. From the first day we could see that their working code disgraced any slacker, and the lack of a foreman to curb their fiercely independent spirits was a distinct advantage. They scrambled up rocky slopes in less than two minutes like goats, when it took the best of us fifteen minutes of cautious climbing to do the same. There were no misgivings on the part of our best men when faced with the task of carrying out heavy pots a meter high and nearly as wide to the car five kilometers away. One of these, by the way, was the famous Muhammed edh-Dhib Hassan, who began the search for manuscripts by throwing a stone into Qumrân Cave I in 1947 (and thus contributed indirectly to the discovery of the Samaria Papyri). As compared with these sturdy men, after two weeks of coming out of Cave II for about 20 meters in a crouched position, I felt ready to join the Old Stone Age men to whom the hunched posture was quite normal--especially with the prospect of a longer campaign there this fall if funds are forthcoming.

Jerusalem - March 14, 1964[2]

At the end of the two-week clearance in the Wâdī ed-Dâliyeh caves in January, 1963, we sealed the caves and set a watch. Ten days later came a report that a leading Ta'âmireh digger with five friends had hired a taxi from Jericho to Mughayir, the nearest village west of the caves. From a visit to the caves about a week later we learned that many more than six Ta'âmireh must have been digging in Cave II in their usual frenetic manner. While we sealed the cave again with a feeling of futility, improved surveillance supported by sporadic army reconnaissance kept further treasure-hunting to a minimum. To the credit of the Ta'âmireh code of honor it should be noted that no digging was carried on near our operations and the piles of bones we had sealed inside Cave I were left undisturbed.

Perhaps our expectation of a painful operation had something to do with the double postponement of this year's cave clearance. We had originally hoped to begin shortly after the fall trip, but a tired lack of enthusiasm was among the reasons for setting the date ahead to the latter part of January. Then illness caused further delay until 3 February, when our operation actually began. Our imported staff of twelve had the support of over fifty workers in a campaign which we completed in just under three weeks. Our non-Arab staff consisted of Fellows George Nickelsburg, Jr., and John M. Holt, Honorary Associate C. Umhau Wolf, and Dr. Siegfried Mittmann as supervisors with the writer serving as director. The Arab staff was composed of Muhammed Abu 'Ajamiyeh, who represented the Department of Antiquities; Corp. Minwar Yaqub Haddad, operator of the mine detector; Aboud Dhib Nasif, driver-mechanic-supervisor; Muhammed Adawi, cook; and our skilled diggers Nasir Diab Mansoor, Muhammed Musa Awadh, and Jabr Muhammed Hassan.

Since this winter has been as wet as the last was dry, we decided to set our camp some distance west of the caves in an open field. This was our greatest mistake. The first night about midnight heavy winds roused us to pound our tent stakes further into the red clay in a driving rain. The next night the winds were worse, and by breakfast time had reached such velocity (over 65 mph) that we were forced to break camp in a hurry to keep serious ripping of tents to a minimum. We retreated to the sheltered Cave II area where we had camped last season and got two tents up before the rains came. The Arab staff slept in Cave II that night. The rest of the staff, after a night in a tent resting on mud, moved into a cave on the opposite side of the wadi. To a man the staff cheerfully made the best of conditions and were consoled by the fact that they were living in warmer quarters than the Jerusalem School provided. The actual excavating conditions were slightly improved over last year with the introduction of electricity into both caves by generators brought in by camel.

Through wind and rain work proceeded normally in Caves I and III, and only half a day was lost in Cave II. Cave I, you may recall, was the cave in which the Samaria Papyri were found, and Cave II was the source of our Middle Bronze I finds. Cave III was the Mugharet ed-Dâliyeh, about a mile west of Cave II at the head of Wâdî ed-Dâliyeh. Just north of it was Cave IV, and nothing of importance was found in either of the new caves. Cursory examination of a number of other caves convinced us that our efforts should again be concentrated on Caves I and II.

In Cave I we undertook limited clearance operations along the trench to the Manuscript Area and in the Bat Dome and Hot Room, (Pl. 8), but our main task was sifting through the remaining debris in the Manuscript Area. This tedious operation produced few surprises: more of the sherds, broken bones, tatters of cloth, sticks, pits, and seeds we had become so familiar with last season, but the pieces seemed even smaller. We were somewhat encouraged by the few beads which turned up almost daily, a fibula, two bullae, and almost daily papyrus bits with hints of a letter or two. As we were nearing the end, the prize find turned up, a larger papyrus fragment with six lines of text containing as many as eight letters in a line--apparently the only larger fragment missed by the Ta'âmireh.

After the Manuscript Area was finished, we shifted our efforts to the passage between the Manuscript Area and the Bat Dome. Here one of our men claimed to have found five silver coins. Significantly, his description of them matches the coins offered for sale with the Samaria Papyri. Here we got still more material familiar from the Manuscript Area--plus a single tiny silver coin spotted by Muhammed Abu 'Azamiyeh. It is of the Philisto-Arabian type, undoubtedly contemporary with the other finds.

There seems to be nothing to change the conclusions of the first season about the fate of the Samaritans. Two independent reports from early diggers at the cave agree that some of the skeletons in the Manuscript Area were originally covered by mats and not lying upon them. A piece of cloth seems to be still adhering to one of the skull fragments. Certainly, this was neither a bone repository nor a traditional burial ground. The mat coverings might have been the last tender act by survivors of the catastrophe, and the relative scarcity of artifacts might be related to the same event.

In Cave II, as we hoped, we more than doubled the number of large Middle Bronze I jars when we cleared the other half of the first inner room. In addition to these seventeen large jars and cooking pots, this season we found parts of several more fine carinated bowls and two nearly complete caliciform vessels. The last are especially important since closely parallel sherds appeared in our Middle Bronze I cemetery clearance last fall.[3] There was practically nothing but pottery in the cave-room except a few bronze toggle pins.

The systematic clearance of the next room inside Cave II did produce some surprises. On the very first day of digging in this area, which seemed almost hopelessly torn up by the Ta'âmireh, a group of six daggers or keys with wooden handles preserved, a handle of a bronze jug, and a pile of 96 beads turned up. Baskets of pottery came from this room to the mouth of the cave in rapid succession. The sherds soon made it clear that we were dealing with an important occupation of the cave in the second century A.D., with material to be assigned to the time of the Second Jewish Revolt. This was further confirmed by the parallels, which Fellow Nickelsburg found from Muraba'ât and Masada, for the bronze jug handle, the iron knife or key group, as well as a wooden bowl and wooden combs. Typically, most of the sherds are from common ovoid store jars, with a few bowls, jugs, and cooking pots represented. Three of the jars are inscribed, one with Hebrew, another with Greek, and a third probably with a potter's marks. Also from this room came the largest and best made of all the Middle Bronze I jars.

At the beginning of the third week, our objectives were nearly accomplished, and it appeared that we would be able to get away a day or two earlier than planned. Several of our Ta'âmireh friends did not like the prospect of losing a good job so soon, and Muhammed Musa undertook the job of trying to convince me that there were still many potential treasure spots in Cave II which had not yet been explored. Several of these I already knew about, but they did not seem especially attractive. They were too damp for manuscripts; there were very few sherds, but, of course, a coin hoard might be found. Then the two of us squirmed on our bellies into a small room through a passage too small for the third and larger member of our group to come along. This room had a good scattering of sherds from the second century A.D. We repeated the squirming process, entering a second room with similar pottery. A passage led to another room with the same sherds and no exit, but another passage led to a larger room, then to a fifth and sixth room each time increasing in size. The sixth was a fairly large cavern in which we could walk around to explore its nooks and crannies. We did not linger long here, for Muhammed found a shaft which led to an underground wadi which extended as far as our spotlights pene- trated in either direction. Making our way down the passage was far from pleasant. The bats were hanging in layers on the walls, and Muhammed and I alternated shrieks when they landed on us. After what seemed like a kilometer but was probably only a couple of city blocks the passage narrowed, and we passed through a tiny opening into a cavern in which a football stadium could have fitted. The air was warm and humid enough to keep the rocks slippery. We began to explore the passages off the cavern, but we were afraid to go too far in any of them. When we were ready to go back, Muhammed had lost his sense of direction and rushed about frantically searching for the tiny exit. Finally, when he slipped and hurt his leg, he became more composed, and I was able to make a systematic search, which led to the exit in a few minutes. We had not made a new discovery. There was scattered evidence of recent digging, and a few sherds and bones here and there told us that this underground labyrinth was known in the second century A.D. By now we were only concerned with getting out, and it was quite a relief to get back to the familiar part of the cave after over two hours of exploring.

Far from luring to more work in Cave II, this adventure convinced me that, aside from clearing the first few small rooms, we should turn the whole thing over to the Ta'âmireh or anyone else whose spirit of adventure would be less easily dampened than mine. Muhammed must have felt the same, for he was here a few days ago asking for work. So we left the caves open when we left. We were not sure that all important finds had been made, but we were convinced that it would be much more safe and sensible to pay off a lucky adventurer than to continue the search. So far this decision has proved a happy one, for from the large-scale digging which commenced upon our departure have come only two blurred bullae and a few beads.

Work on the cave materials commenced in earnest almost immediately upon our return to Jerusalem. Fellow Nickelsburg is documenting parallels for the Second Revolt material and supervising mending of the contemporary pottery. He has the help of Mr. and Mrs. Malcolm Lyall-Watson as well as part-time assistance from Mrs. Bernhard Anderson and her son Ronald. Mr. Lyall-Watson is on his way back to South Africa after completing a doctorate in zoology in England.

Through the facilitation of James Swauger, Assistant Director of the Carnegie Museum in Pittsburgh, and the courtesy of W. M. Krogman, Director of the Philadelphia Center for Research in Child Growth, it has been possible to secure Mr. Mahinder Sain Chopra to study the Wâdî ed-Dâliyeh skeletal remains. Mr. Chopra has been at work almost constantly since his arrival: sorting, measuring, and selecting bones for X-ray, photography, and casts. He has been discussing pathological matters with Dr. Vicken Kalbian, who is also kindly arranging for X-ray facilities. All that can be reported at this time is that some 160 men, women, and children are represented by the bones from the Manuscript Area alone.

Chapter VII

THE MIRZBÂNEH CEMETERY

Jerusalem, Jordan, October 8, 1963[1]

Shortly after the Wâdî ed-Dâliyeh cave clearance last January,
we decided to check on the effectiveness of our watchmen and
explore the six-kilometer path west from the caves to the village
of Mughâyir. Villagers from there farmed land near the caves, and
several of them had visited the dig, inquiring about employment
and describing antiquities in the vicinity of their village. Of
special interest was a large Middle Bronze I tomb group brought to
the dig by two lads. They claimed it came from near the village
and, surprisingly, with the purchase agreed to lead us to the find
spot at a convenient time.

On 6 February American Consul General and Mrs. William Hamilton
and the Lapp family got an early start on an overnight camping trip
to Mughâyir. Leaving our driver and small daughter to set up camp
near the village, we hiked east to the caves. At the caves we
learned that our surveillance system needed improvement and on the
way back--uphill all the way--that the more precipitous approach
to the caves from the east was shorter and less tiring. The next
day we were shown the antiquities of the village, rock-cut Roman
tombs, some apparently still undisturbed, being the most interesting. Then our two guides took us back to the Nablus Road, south
to the Taiyibeh Road, and down to 'Ain es-Sâmiyeh. From there a
kilometer walk up the Wâdî Sîya' brought us to the site of the
tomb find--a long trip to arrive at a point only two kilometers
SSW of Mughâyir (Pl. 11).

What we saw was quite exciting--dozens of round shafts
averaging about four feet in diameter--some of them with telltale
piles of dirt nearby but most of them apparently undisturbed.
This was obviously the vicinity from which MB I material had been
turning up in Jerusalem for some time.[2] The young diggers opened
the small entrances only enough to permit squirming into the tomb
chambers from the shafts. I was persuaded to wriggle into the
purported chamber of the tomb group, and both the freshness of
the dirt outside and impressions of vessels on the floor inside
seemed to corroborate the claim. The situation was complicated
by the fact, as we later discovered, that later chambers were cut
into earlier ones so that we examined three additional chambers
by crawling through larger and smaller cavities. At that point
it seemed clear that some tombs of this cemetery should be cleared
by scientific excavation in the fall in relation to the MB I cave
discovery at Wâdî ed-Dâliyeh. On emerging from this tomb we were
taken about 300 feet down the slope to another area dotted with

77

round shafts, another cemetery. Indeed, our guide wanted to
show us a third and a fourth, but our time was running out.

Plans did materialize for a fall campaign, and we were able
to investigate and plan some thirty of the tombs rather carefully between 2 and 21 September. The undertaking was made possible
by the willingness of Taanach's architect, David Voelter, to pro-
long his stay to serve as our architect. Field supervisors included Fellow John Holt, Professor Delbert Flora, and Mr. Yasushi
Ogawa. Our technical men, Nasir Diab from Balâtah, Muhammed
Ibrahim Hussein and Abdul Rahman Hussein of Ta'annek, and Muhammed
Musa Awadh of Bethlehem, served as the backbone of our staff; Mr.
Amin Baroum represented the Jordan Department of Antiquities; and
Aboud Dhib Nasif served as driver, supervisor, and mechanic for the
generators. The writer served as director and photographer. We
were able to commute daily to the site from Jerusalem, leaving the
technical men encamped, two in each of the cemeteries under excavation.

When we arrived for the first day's work, we found the camp
in order, all equipment on hand, and a group of twenty-six workers
(recruited from Kufr Malik through the courtesy of the District
Commander) ready to dig. After appointing a watchman and waterman,
we selected six four-man teams, three to work in the upper and
three in the lower cemetery. The procedure for selecting tombs
for excavation was not rigorous. We tried to avoid tombs that
might have been robbed and looked for the least-eroded spots on
the limestone shelves. The choice was rather fortunate, but this
we did not discover for some days.

As the teams began clearing the first shafts, we began plotting
the circular shafts visible from the surface. Only a single tree
could be seen from the cemeteries, and it was some distance away.
The landscape consisted of shelves of limestone rising in terraces
for wadi beds with thin patches of red clay here and there nourish-
ing scrubby plant life (Pl. 11). The limestone varied considerably
in hardness, and the shelves were honeycombed with caves. It was
along shelves of softer limestone (nari) that the tools of the
tomb-diggers were effective. In one instance a beautiful shaft was
cut in softer stone only to be abandoned when stone even too hard
for our modern tools was encountered. By the end of the dig we
had plotted 48 shafts in lower Cemetery A and 38 in upper Cemeteries
B and C. Careful cleaning of bedrock would have revealed more. In
fact, at the end of the dig we reached several chambers for whose
shafts we had not time to search.

We had hoped a pattern of opening two or three tombs a day
would emerge so that photography, planning, and recording could
proceed at an even pace. After the first few minutes of digging
it became clear that this would not be possible. Just below the
surface most of the shafts were packed with extremely hard lime
earth or huwar which was sometimes almost impossible to distinguish

from the limestone shell containing it. It took an ambitious
team an average of three and a half days to clear a shaft eleven
feet deep, and the effort was probably not much less than
cutting one originally. A few shafts were more lightly packed
with coarse red earth, and these were easier to clear. Tomb
chambers reached through such shafts were completely empty, so
we concluded that this was a temporary packing to preserve the
chamber until it was needed.

The diggers were always gratified when a large boulder or
semidressed stone began to appear in the shaft (Pl. 12). This
meant that the base of the shaft was near (frequently nearly three
feet down, the length of the blocking stone), and there were
prospects of an untouched tomb. More often than not they were
disappointed, for behind the blocking stone the chambers were
commonly filled with rockfall and silt, and this meant perhaps
another week before the chamber could be cleared. The fill in
the shafts and the fall in the chambers was usually sterile
except for occasional MB I sherds (plus one or two Byzantine
sherds near the surface). This added up to long hours of un-
romantic archaeology or dirt removal. In fact, at the end of our
first week we had practically nothing else to report--not a single
whole pot or exciting artifact. Perhaps all the tombs had either
been robbed in ancient or modern times or were so covered by fallen
rock and silt that the few pots which might be lying below were
not worth the effort to reach them! This, at least, probably ex-
plained why our two young friends had no hesitation about leading
us to the site.

Early in the second week we learned that removing the some
thirty tons of debris from filled chambers would not go completely
unrewarded, for Tomb A-4 (Pl. 12) produced a whole and several
restorable pots and a pile of bones under tons of silt and rockfall. Later in the week we found our first undisturbed tomb, A-41.
Peering through the cracks between the walls and the blocking stone
we could see some of the pots just as they had been left nearly
4000 years ago. None of the other "clean" tombs subsequently discovered was more exciting than this one, so it may be well to describe it in some detail (Pl. 13).

The shaft, cut into a wide, flat shelf of soft limestone, was
some eleven feet deep and had an average diameter of somewhat
under four feet. It was quite circular and very well-cut. Except
for the top foot, the shaft was filled with extremely hardpacked
sterile huwar. The stone blocking the entrance was a rough limestone slab 30" x 28" x 8" thick. It effectively blocked the
entryway, and small stones chinked the gaps. Inside, two thin
layers covered the floor. Upon the floor was a thin layer of
soft earth less than an inch thick upon which the bones and artifacts lay. This layer had either been deposited during the

interval between cutting and use of the tomb or, more likely, had
been spread by the buriers to provide a bed on which to place the
bones (a practice with modern local parallels). On this lay some
two inches of very fine dust in which were bedded some small
chips of roof fall. After removing this layer we could see the
chamber just as it had been left by those who set the stone and
filled the shaft.

The chamber is kidney-shaped with a diameter of 15 feet.
The central height of the chamber is four feet, with roof tapering
gradually to a nearly vertical sidewall. The tool marks of the
tomb-cutters were apparent in the roof, hack marks made by a
picking tool with a sharpened head about 3/4 of an inch thick--
quite similar to the tools used by our workmen except that in
those days they were made of bronze. The tomb contained the
bones of at least three persons. Leg bone fragments of one
individual were lying just inside the tomb entrance near the wall
to the right. Farther back along the wall to the right the
larger bones and skull of a second individual were laid with
little reference to their original articulation. The cap of the
skull had fallen away, and two lower jaws lay nearby. The third
person was represented by a third group of leg bones similar to
the first near the wall opposite the entrance. The second not
only had more of his bones interred but had a well-preserved
bronze dagger and pin with curled over head and two, possibly
three, small pots associated with him.

Other pottery vessels were scattered around the tomb--two
four-spouted lamps, five other small jars or cups, a two-handled
small pot, and a large jar with envelope ledge handles. Some of
these jars were sitting properly and had collected the same dust
which sifted down on the floor; others were scattered in various
positions, the whole group giving the impression of careless,
hurried placement, certainly when compared to the care and effort
with which the chamber was cut.

Other tombs, excluding of course those which had not been
used, provided the same general picture. One (A-14, see Pl. 14)
had two skulls lying toward the right rear of the chamber with
seven of the common flared-rim cups scattered around and against
one of the skulls. There were a few larger bones near the center
of the tomb, and four lamps (one upside down), six more cups, and
the base of a large jar were scattered about. Another had a heap
of bones and skull fragments at the back of the chamber with 15
lamps and vessels piled on the bones. Near the mid-left side of
the chamber were fragments of leg bones, arm bones, and a skull
placed above each other in that order, and just to the right of
the entrance were four more flared cups. We found no articulated
burials, and no small bones such as fingers and toes were discovered in any of the tombs.

The interpretation of this evidence is rather difficult.
Certainly, great effort was taken to see that the large bones of
at least certain members of a community or tribe were sealed in
a rockcut tomb chamber. It is quite possible that the preparation
of the chamber was supervised by the deceased before his death,
for there are three clear examples of lightly packed shaft fills
blocking unused chambers. The number of bones preserved for burial
and their particular placement were apparently unimportant. Tomb
gifts were not essential, for two undisturbed chambers contained
only bones. Upside down cups, jars, and lamps in others suggest
that there was no concern to provide a food supply for the deceased.
The dagger may have been to aid the deceased in his future struggles,
but this seems doubtful in light of the fact that daggers are
characteristic of only one of the several tomb types of this period
at other sites. In fact, the disposition of vases in the tombs
suggests that they were carelessly left behind after use by the
buriers.

If we ask about the community that created the cemetery, our
evidence fits with that from contemporary sites in Palestine.
This evidence has led scholars to consider Middle Bronze I (2100-
1900 B.C.) a period when seminomadic tribal troups invaded the
country. Their incursion left Palestine almost completely without
centers of sedentary occupation, as campsite occupation in this
period on major tells indicates. The fact that relatively few
bones and none of the smallest ones were placed in our tombs could
suggest that the corpses had been left to decay on roofs or enclosures, but more fitting seems a seminomadic background in which
the tribe returned once or twice each year to its burial ground
carrying back the few bones that managed to survive in their saddle-
bags. In fact, the top of the barren ridge with the lower cemetery
on its slopes has vestiges of a campsite with fragments of contemporary MB pottery and hundreds of curious cupped depressions in the
rock. Certainly, the tribesmen would have moved their flocks far
from here for pasturage in the dry season. The fact that each
chamber contained one chief burial could be interpreted as an indication that clan chiefs within the tribe were accorded such
burial, and the few bones of other burials might represent favorite
sons, wives, or servants.

The evidence provides little help in determining the cultic
beliefs and practices associated with the burials. The apparent
concern to be buried with "his fathers" does not imply any kind of
belief in an afterlife, and there is no clear evidence of an attempt
to provide provision for the future of the deceased. The careless
or hurried way in which the bones and artifacts were deposited could
imply some terror associated with the deposition of the bones, but
this seems unlikely for bones which had probably become familiar
traveling companions. More likely perhaps is the possibility that

some ritual was celebrated in the tomb just before it was closed--
maybe including strong drink from the cups common in these
chambers. About this we can only guess until literary evidence
becomes available.[3]

Chapter VIII

THE SALVAGE EXCAVATION AT TELL EL-FÛL

Jerusalem, Jordan, June 14, 1964[1]

Yesterday he finished a six-week campaign at Tell el-Fûl.
W. F. Albright conducted his first archaeological campaign here
in 1922-23 and we followed up with a second campaign in 1933.[2]
The third campaign became a possibility when James L. Kelso
wrote to inquire if there was interest in the Jerusalem School
continuing its tradition of joint excavations with Pittsburgh
Theological Seminary. He expressed interest in a site near
Jerusalem which had Hellenistic and Early Roman remains. My
suggestion of a campaign at Tell el-Fûl was welcomed by Professor
Kelso and enthusiastically supported by Professor Albright, who
has provided helpful counsel and the original plans from the
earlier campaigns.

Tell el-Fûl was on my list of sites in Jordan deserving
prompt archaeological attention. The western slope is rapidly
being covered with beautiful new homes, and at the present rapid
building pace the mound will be covered within a few years. King
Hussein has rented one of these homes as his West Bank palace.
Press reports indicate that he may erect a palace at the summit,
but apparently there are no immediate plans. In any case, there
seemed some justification in considering the campaign a salvage
operation.

Was there anything at Tell el-Fûl worth salvaging? An
examination of the balks of the modern trenches which traverse
the mound and its slopes suggested a negative answer. Except
for limited areas on the east, there was no evidence of ancient
occupation on the slopes, and most of the summit, as our east-west
trench across the summit subsequently proved, was covered by a
deposit of a half-meter or less. Only to the north of the
previously excavated fortress area and on the eastern slope was
there a prospect of some depth of stratification, unless one
would consider moving the large dump of the earlier campaigns
on the east side of the fortress. As we laid out the plots for
excavation on 3 May to the north of the fortress area (Pl. 15)
and north of the previous excavation on the east side, Albright's
conclusion at the end of the 1933 campaign was ringing in my ears:
"It is hardly probable that the returns would warrant another
campaign." From surface observations, it seemed that we would
certainly substantiate his judgment.

Why not then be content with the conclusions of the earlier
excavations and turn to a site with better prospects? This was

impossible, first, because highly reputable scholars were quite
doubtful about the earlier conclusions. The proposed reconstruction
of Saul's fort has been opposed in detail or in toto. One serious
Palestinian excavator who had studied in England seriously suggested
before the excavation that we would discover that Saul's fort was
Hellenistic. Such reactions are understandable in light of Dr.
Kenyon's discoveries about the millennial mis-datings of "Joshua's"
walls at Jericho and the "Jebusite" and "Davidic" walls at Ophel.
Could Albright's conclusions be trusted more than those of his
contemporaries?

The limitations of the final report of the second campaign are
certainly related to the skepticism expressed about the conclusions
and were also an important factor urging further excavation. Only
about ten pages of text describe the constructions unearthed in
the second campaign, and much of what is represented in the plans
is not described at all. In the Hellenistic pottery discussion
hardly a single form in the so-called third century B.C. group could
be assigned such a date. Most of the pottery saved from the 1933
campaign, which is at the Jerusalem School, was not studied for the
final publication. In light of reaction to the final report of the
second campaign--especially outside the United States--it seemed
clear that the American School had not yet fulfilled its reporting
obligations at Tell el-Fûl. This seemed true despite the fact that
some criticism of the report, based on the tacit assumption that
the site had been excavated in the 1960's rather than the 1930's,
was unfair.

In a word, the results of the campaign provide a remarkable
confirmation of Albright's conclusions--those of the first campaign
somewhat more than those of the second. The accuracy of his conclusions as compared with those of his contemporaries is amazing.
To check on his results we excavated a trench from the west against
the northwest corner of what Albright called the tower of Saul's
fortress (Pl. 16). Its foundation trench contained pottery of the
post-Philistine phase of Iron I. Strata lying against the buttress-
ing of the west face of the tower contained the same pottery and
should be considered a repair during its Iron I use. The ceramic
chronology of this period is not precise enough to propose a dating
closer than between the last quarter of the 11th and mid-10th
centuries B.C. While it is therefore not categorically proved
that the fortress belonged to Saul, the identification rests on
evidence about as strong as archaeology is ever able to provide--
especially in light of the comparably strong case for the identification of Tell el-Fûl with Gibeah of Saul. In fact, no rival
hypothesis of any substance has been proposed, and the evidence
upon which Albright based his identification of 1922-23 stands
confirmed.

In the same trench a portion of the sloping revetment, which
Albright attributed to the latter part of Iron II, was dismantled.

The pottery from the dismantling confirms his results and conclusions. Only slight modification is required in that this
pottery can be more precisely assigned to the late 7th-early 6th
century B.C. horizon rather than the 8th-7th century B.C. A
poorly constructed banking west of the revetment, not dated in
the earlier reports, belongs to the hurried Hellenistic repair
of the defenses at the time of the Maccabees.

Perhaps the most controversial issue arising from the
earlier campaigns centers around Albright's proposed reconstruction
of Saul's fortress. It has been objected that the contours of the
mound preclude the extension of the fort eastward as far as the
reconstruction necessitates, and it has been felt by some scholars
that Saul had only a defensive tower, not a larger fort at Tell
el-Fûl. New light on this problem was unearthed north of the
tower area in the form of a three-meter fragment of the west wall
of Saul's fort (Pl. 16). Its attribution to the fort is assured:
it is nearly on a line with the west wall extending north from the
southwest tower previously excavated; it is the same 1.50 meter
width; it has strata of earth against it on each side containing
exclusively what we have called the 1000 B.C. pottery horizon.
Albright's view, that Saul had not merely a tower but a fort here,
is vindicated. Under the wall was a .30 meter layer of clay on
bedrock, corresponding to the pre-fortress phase reported by
Albright in the tower area.

Yet, his views do need modification. The wall fragment just
mentioned extends north of the north wall of the fort according
to Albright's reconstruction.[3] This shows that the north-south
axis of the fort was longer than Albright proposed, and it may be
considered a hint that the longer axis of the fort, as the contours
of the mound would tend to indicate, was the north-south one, not
the east-west as Albright proposed. According to Albright, the
rectangular fort was of the casemate type. It is clear that there
was no wall in the preserved Iron I debris east of our wall fragment to correspond to the inner wall of the casemate. Accordingly,
as Albright has agreed in subsequent private correspondence, the
view that Saul's fort was a casemate must be abandoned.

The preservation of a small segment of the fort's west wall
was quite fortuitous. Between this segment and the tower Iron II
operations had cleared the entire area to bedrock, and to the
north Hellenistic constructions rested on the natural surface of
the tell. The only other traces of Iron I occupation appeared
on the eastern edge of the summit. Here, a silt deposit on the
floor of a silo and a pocket in a deeply excavated cavity in
bedrock contained pure Iron I pottery. The pottery of the pre-
fortress phase indicates an occupation in the first half of the
12th century B.C. while the pottery associated with the fortress
belongs to the period of about 1025-950 B.C. There seems to have
been a definite gap in occupation during the period of the Philistine

ascendancy, and there seems to be no evidence to recommend the view that Saul's fort had been originally a Philistine construction.

Gibeah was a strongly fortified site in the last decades of the Iron II period, and its population seems to have increased substantially as the sixth century progressed. To the strategic revetted tower unearthed in the earlier campaigns two new defensive elements may be added. The first is an Iron II casemate. This has been keyed into the lowest courses of the north face of the revetment, which, it may be recalled, enclosed the southwest tower of the fortress of Saul. The .80 meter outer wall is separated from the .50 meter inner wall (see Pl. 16) by an intersice of about 1.50 meters. At the north end of our excavation along the east edge of the summit appeared another portion of what could be presumed to be the same casemate because of its closely parallel dimensions and type of construction. The inner wall of the casemate was traced without a break for over 20 meters along the eastern edge of the summit and presumably continues south immediately to the east of Albright's 1933 excavations. The outer wall was founded on bedrock and in places was built against a vertical face cut into bedrock. Its width varied between .75 and 1.35 meters because of the packing of its inner phase against sloping bedrock. In the few places it was preserved above foundation in our excavations it was some .80 meters thick. This is the first casemate to be excavated in Palestine from so late in the Iron II period, but the evidence for its dating seems incontrovertible.

Only a tiny vestige of the other new Iron II defensive element was preserved. This was a sloping revetment to the east of the casemate, preserved to a height of four courses in one spot, elsewhere to a height of only one or two miserable courses resting on bedrock. Farther down the eastern slope were remains of an attempt to shore up this revetment. It is tempting to suggest that there was a revetted tower similar to the one at the southwest on the northeastern corner of the summit, but the vestiges so far unearthed make it impossible to go beyond suggestion. Further excavation in the northeast corner of the summit would be desirable.

A few additional fragmentary Iron II remains may be noted. Inside the east casemate was the corner of a well-built Iron II building with foundations cut nearly a meter into bedrock and a meter thick. Fragments of the floor associated with this building had over 20 cm. of ashy destruction debris upon it. This is the only evidence of the 1964 campaign to be connected with the earlier evidence that this occupation ended with destruction. A few of the silos and a cistern had layers of silt containing pure Iron II pottery on their floors, notably a silo near the center of the mound and a cistern within the casemate on the west side.

After the destruction of Tell el-Fûl, presumably during Nebuchadnezzar's campaign of 597 B.C., the site soon became quite

heavily populated again as the huge quantities of pottery from
the mid-sixth century B.C. testify. In our excavations to the
northwest we discovered a large, well-plastered cistern (Pl. 17)
divided in half by a partition wall containing, at the floor, a
passageway 1.70 meters high between the two halves. (Only half
the cistern was excavated, and the similarity of the two halves
is merely an assumption.) The cistern is cut 5.25 meters into
bedrock and has a maximum diameter of 4.95 meters. From the
debris which filled it came 93 full baskets of pottery and not
a few objects. Most important was the lowest silt layer which
contained 49 baskets of pottery forming a homogeneous group to
be assigned approximately to the middle of the sixth century B.C.
Other clear evidence of mid-sixth century occupation came from
the area west of the west casemate. Here were substantial walls
laid on bedrock but of smaller stones than those of Iron II
proper. Peaceful conditions seem to have prompted occupation
outside the still-standing Iron II defenses.

The end of this occupation is difficult to specify precisely,
but it must have been sometime in the second half of the sixth
century B.C. It is interesting to note that Gibeon, Bethel, and
Shechem seem to have been abandoned about the same time.[4] There
seems to be no satisfactory historical explanation of these facts
though the abandonment of these sites is apparently not associated
with any destruction. To be especially noted is the apparent
prosperity of these towns in the late sixth century in marked contrast with evidence from sites excavated to the south of Jerusalem.
In any case, our results point to a strongly fortified town in
the latter part of the Iron II period which continued to prosper
for something like a half century after the Babylonian destruction.

After this abandonment the site lay unoccupied until the latter
part of the third century B.C. and then became a populous Hellenistic town during the last half of the second century B.C. The
vestiges of Hellenistic occupation before about 165 B.C. recovered
in this campaign were minimal, and examination of the pottery at
the American School in Jerusalem suggests a similar result for the
earlier campaigns. This contradicts the judgment of the final
publication of the second campaign that "there is no evidence that
the mound was occupied during the period of the Maccabees, as it
was first thought; instead it lay in ruins during the second and
part of the first century B.C." Actually, the second century B.C.
was one of the site's most flourishing centuries, as Albright
already recognized after the first campaign. It is difficult to
decide about the extent of the late third century occupation since
it is possible that here was a substantial occupation which was
swept away in the second century B.C. But since these operations
left fragments in pockets of Iron I, Iron II, and sixth century
occupation, the lack of something comparable from the third century

suggests that occupation was slight until the second quarter of
the second century B.C.

The 175 B.C. ceramic horizon is clearly represented in the
bottom of one silo group from the east side excavation, and on
the west in another silo and in relation to a doorway and a few
other vestiges of construction on bedrock nearby. These
structures are composed of rectangular blocks of soft limestone,
many of which are reused in later Hellenistic walls. These later
walls comprise two clearly distinct phases of the east side, and
a two-meter thick wall on the west side with its subsequent re-
build. A good series of Hellenistic floors is to be associated
with the later phase on the west side, and a floor of each phase
is preserved over large areas of the eastern plot. The end of
Hellenistic occupation is difficult to specify precisely. It
probably came about 100 B.C. In any case, the Hellenistic
occupation belongs substantially to the last two-thirds of the
second century B.C.

On the east side the earlier of the well-preserved Hellenistic phases cleared out, repaired, and added an interior buttress
to the Iron II casemate. To the west of the casemate bedrock was
shaved away so that the western ends of the Hellenistic rooms are
partially hollowed out of bedrock. In the later phase the casemate is filled with rubble and a new wall line over a meter to
the west of the casemate delimits the eastern edge of the town.
As in the case of the inner casemate wall, this line could be
traced all along the eastern edge of our excavations for over 20
meters. The two-meter wall on the west must have originally
served some defensive purpose but as we found it, it had what
were apparently domestic floors on both sides. It may be presumed
originally to have extended north from the Hellenistic tower of
the earlier excavations but had been subsequently robbed by later
Hellenistic builders. The later Hellenistic phase on the west
side consisted of several well-preserved rooms with intact floors--
occasionally with complete Hellenistic vessels still resting on
them. A curious plaster installation from this phase was built
against the north face of the Iron II revetment. It consisted of
four quarters, each something over a meter square separated by
partitions and connected by drains (Pl. 18). The installation
seems too complicated to have been merely a series of settling
basins, and perhaps the installation should be related to a dyeing
industry.

Other periods of occupation were represented by a few sherds
only. There was one sherd only which could be clearly assigned to
Early Bronze III from the eastern excavations and a few early
Middle Bronze II sherds around a flint outcrop at the northwest
corner of the summit. The latter included the well-known cooking
pots with holes pierced through just below the rim. The Early
Roman period was represented by a few sherds from the surface

layers at the eastern and western edges of the summit. The few
lamp nozzles, jar rims, and coins recovered this season could
easily have been left by the soldiers of Titus, who camped at
the site before they reached Jerusalem in A.D. 70. No structures
could be assigned to these periods. We found nothing like the
abundance of first century B.C.-first century A.D. pottery reported from the earlier campaigns. Perhaps this was actually
pottery from the 100 B.C. horizon, or perhaps there had been an
isolated Early Roman installation just north of the north face
of the Iron II revetment which had been completely removed by
the earlier excavations.

Nearly all the 24 silos cleared had been used in the
Hellenistic period. It has been suggested that the numerous
silos in the east side of the mound are quite similar to the
large number discovered at el-Jîb which have there been associated
with a wine industry. This campaign produced no evidence that any
of the silos were so used. In most cases there is no direct evidence for determining whether a silo was cut in the Hellenistic
or Iron age. One silo had been used in the Iron I period, and
another had been cut before an Iron II wall was built over it.
Another had a mid-second century B.C. wall built over its mouth,
and others had good end of Iron II and late 6th century pottery
groups in deposits on their floors. Most of the silos are quite
similar in shape. Some were capped by well-cut round stone lids,
others by capstones with plugs fitting into the small mouth of
the shaft. The larger-mouthed silos with round drum-like stone
caps probably were originally used in the Iron I period while
those with small openings capped by plug lids seem to have been
cut in the Iron II period. It seems doubtful that any of the
silos were originally Hellenistic. The silos were undoubtedly
standard equipment for the Iron age house, for storing grain and
large jars containing oil, wine, or water. Even some of those
from el-Jîb were quite probably used for such ordinary purposes.

We came upon only two plastered cisterns. The silos had no
plaster except that in a couple of instances natural cavities in
bedrock were filled with stones and cracks with sherds and the
cavity then covered with a layer of mortar. This was presumably
to keep out rodents or moisture. The two well-plastered cisterns,
the larger having been described above, were both considerably
larger than the silos. Both had 6th century B.C. deposits on
their floors and were later reused in the Hellenistic period. A
well-preserved channel was associated with the smaller one.

The object registry includes, in addition to about 100
vessels of the late 6th century B.C., 25 coins (mostly Ptolemaic
and Seleucid), six Hellenistic lamps, six 6th century B.C. lamps,
21 well-preserved bone picks and spatulas, eight animal and human
figurine heads and bodies, stamped jar handles, and two jars

bearing Hebrew inscriptions of the late second century B.C.
Most of the objects, with the exception of the coins, came from
the silos and cisterns.

On a mound cleaned to bedrock several times in antiquity
with such a thin occupation deposit left for excavation, we felt
indeed fortunate to have found as many objects and constructions
as we did. That these were excavated in a careful and professional
manner is the result of the dedicated efforts of our staff. This
was composed of Professor James L. Kelso, President; Fellows George
Nickelsburg, Jr., and John Holt, Professors Howard Jamieson and
Delbert Flora, and Drs. C. Umhau Wolf and John Zimmerman, Field
Supervisors; Mr. Oliver Unwin, Architect; Mrs. C. Umhau Wolf,
Registrar; Aboud Dhib Nasif, Driver-Foreman; Nasir Dhiab Mansoor,
Jabr Muhammed Hassan, Muhammed Hussein, and Abd er-Rahman Hussein,
Technical Men; and the undersigned as Director and Photographer.
The work force averaged about 55 workers, who worked eight hours
a day, five days a week.

Two-thirds of the budget of just over $3000 was provided by
Pittsburgh Theological Seminary through the courtesy of Professors
Kelso and Jamieson, and the rest came from the regular archaeological budget of the Jerusalem School. I think it is safe to
conclude that the entire staff agreed with Professor Kelso's judgment upon departure that we had gotten our money's worth!

Chapter IX

TAANACH BY THE WATERS OF MEGIDDO

American School, Jerusalem, Jordan[1]

The frequency of its mention in the Bible is not a very reliable guide to the size or historical importance of a town in biblical times. Taanach is mentioned seven times, Megiddo twelve. The size of Taanach, delimited throughout its history by its Early Bronze fortifications, is nearly fourteen acres. While Megiddo was somewhat larger than Taanach in the Bronze age, in Israelite times Megiddo covered only about thirteen acres. Much more prominent in biblical events are Shiloh and Bethel, mentioned respectively 32 and 64 times. Both these towns are less than a third the size of Taanach.

The differing purposes of the various biblical texts are major factors in determining the number of times a town is mentioned in the Bible. Some towns were mentioned because they happened to be the scene of an important battle or death, or were on a territorial border. Part of the prominence of Shiloh and Bethel undoubtedly comes from their role as centers in which elements of biblical tradition developed. The relative prominence of Megiddo over Taanach may be attributed to the fact that Megiddo was a seat of governmental administration, for this likely accounts for the connection of Ahaziah and Josiah with Megiddo rather than with Taanach.

Aside from the famous battle at Taanach by the waters of Megiddo memorialized in the Song of Deborah (Judges 5:19), Taanach is mentioned in the Bible only as a town undefeated by Joshua (Judges 1:27), in a list of towns with kings smitten by Joshua (Joshua 12:21), in the tribal allotments (Joshua 17:11; I Chron. 7:29[2]), as a Levitical town (Joshua 21:25), and as a town in a Solomonic administrative district (I Kings 4:12). Together these references suggest that although the Canaanites suffered a notable defeat near Taanach in the days of Deborah, Taanach remained a Canaanite stronghold until it came under Solomon's dominion.

Outside the Bible there are four references to Taanach. Two Egyptian reliefs mention victories at Taanach, the first by Tuthmosis III on May 12, 1468 B.C. and the second by Shishak in 918 B.C. Later Taanach appears as an important 4th century A.D. village in Eusebius' Onomasticon and in Crusader records of the 12th and 13th centuries. A possible fifth reference is in Amarna letter No. 248, where an incomplete name may refer to 14th century B.C. Taanach.

The site of ancient Taanach has never been lost. The modern village of some 200 inhabitants, located around the eastern half

of the base of the tell, still bears the name of Ta'annek. Its
location at the southern edge of the rich plain of Esdraelon five
miles southeast of Megiddo corresponds precisely with the geographical indications of the ancient sources. To learn more about
Taanach than the few bits and tatters gleaned from ancient literary records, archaeological investigation was required.

Ta'annek was one of the first sites to attract excavation in
Palestine. It stands at the beginning of the German archaeological
tradition, even before Megiddo and Jericho. Ernst Sellin began
planning for excavation soon after he first saw the tell on April
11, 1899. His plans soon came to fruition with three campaigns
between 1902 and 1904. The excavations produced what might be
considered spectacular results for a Palestinian mound. In his
first campaign he excavated what has proved to be one of the
finest examples of a Bronze age patrician's house yet discovered
in Palestine (the West Building in Pl. 19). He also came upon a
large incense stand filled with exotic reliefs of animals, sphinxes,
a child throttling a snake, and two goats with a tree of life. In
the 1903 campaign the most spectacular find was a group of four
beautifully preserved Akkadian cuneiform tablets. The final short
campaign was undertaken primarily to search for additional tablets.
Three more tablets and six fragments were found in addition to
another room in which was found an interesting set of jewelry with
the skeletal remains of an adult and five children. The cuneiform
cache still constitutes the largest Akkadian tablet group found
in Palestine.

After the prompt and, for its time, respectably thorough
publication of the excavation,[3] Taanach subsequently played a
very minor role in the literature and conversation of Palestinian
archaeologists. A few of its outstanding finds were incorporated
into archaeological handbooks, and there have been isolated articles
on finds such as the Akkadian tablets and the incense stand.

Taanach reappeared prominently in 1960 in discussions of a
number of American scholars as they made plans for an excavation in
Jordan. For them Taanach seemed the most attractive site in all
Jordan. It was a known ancient site with extensive Bronze and
Iron age remains with very little encumbrance by later occupation.
The German excavations had demonstrated the richness of the site,
and some of their finds were of such importance as to merit re-
examination and clarification by further excavation. It was not
surprising to learn subsequently that Kathleen Kenyon had given
careful consideration to Taanach before deciding upon Jerusalem as
the successor to the Jericho excavations.

The American scholars were associated with a number of
Concordia schools of The Lutheran Church-Missouri Synod. In
December, 1961, they formally decided to form an expedition to
Taanach, to attempt to develop the excavation jointly with the

American School of Oriental Research, and to seek funds. The
ASOR agreed to a joint expedition looking toward a first campaign
in the summer of 1963, and funds for the first two campaigns have
been forthcoming from the Aid Association for Lutherans, a Lutheran
insurance company. In addition, grants have been made for core
staff training and student travel by the Missouri Synod.

It was the desire of these scholars to do the best job of
preparation and excavation with the resources available. The
group originally consisted of four members plus the writer. The
three members of the group who had not had field experience plus
an architecture student were accepted as members of the 1962
Shechem expedition staff for field training. The group determined
to try to dig four kinds of material, assigning one member of the
group to each kind. Albert Glock took responsibility for fortifications, Delbert Hillers for domestic and industrial installations,
A. von Rohr Sauer for cultic materials, and Carl Graesser, Jr., for
public buildings. Before the first campaign each scholar was to
present to the excavation staff a summary of the parallel material
in Palestine for his area, and before the second campaign the
parallel material of the entire Near East. For example, before
the first campaign Glock discussed the character and development
of Palestinian town defenses in the Bronze and Iron ages. Before
the second campaign he discussed Bronze and Iron age defenses in
Egypt, Mesopotamia, Anatolia, and Greece with special reference
to their relations to Palestine and the defenses of Taanach. In
addition, Walter Rast assumed responsibility for tombs and discussed
his material during the second campaign.

With this background and after a week of preparatory planning
and lectures, the first campaign at Ta'annek was conducted between
June 17 and August 10, 1963, with a staff of 26 and a labor force
averaging 125. A second campaign with a staff of 33 and a labor
force averaging about 140 was conducted between July 11 and August
26, 1966. A third and final campaign in the series is projected
for the summer of 1968.[4] In general, the excavation of the Iron
age levels has been completed in the first two campaigns, and the
final excavation report on Taanach's Iron age remains is in preparation. The last campaign will concentrate on excavating the Bronze
age levels to bedrock in the areas now opened.

Before turning to the specific results of the excavation it
is a pleasure to take this opportunity to express appreciation to
our Jordanian friends who helped make the expedition's two campaigns so enjoyable. These include our laborers, some of whom
have become quite skilled at stratigraphic excavation; the villagers
of Ta'annek and their able mukhtar, Naif Muhammed; the local civil
and military officials of the Jordan Government; the Jordan Department of Antiquities and its representatives, who made significant

contributions; and those officials who granted or facilitated
the required permissions, of whom at least Col. Awad Khaldi and
Mahmoud Naim must be mentioned.

Occupational History

Until about 2700 B.C. Tell Ta'annek was a rather bare and
somewhat isolated rocky outcrop at the southern edge of the
Esdraelon plain. Its first substantial occupation involved a
major planning and construction project. The entire outcrop was
lined with a thick, small-stone defense wall, and vast fills were
imported to level the area incorporated into the town. These
operations determined the defense lines and size of the town
through its Bronze and Iron age history. For something over two
centuries Taanach was a very active, thriving town as attested by
its many fortification repairs and rebuilds and by the intricate
stratigraphy of the town occupation. About the middle of the 3rd
millennium B.C. Taanach, like neighboring Megiddo, was abandoned--
under what circumstances has yet to be determined. In this phase
Taanach was a typical town of the Early Bronze "city-state" system,
clearly linked to its neighbors by its ceramic repertory including
Khirbet Kerak ware.

So far the excavations have uncovered no evidence of town
life for the next eight centuries. During much of this time town
life ceased to exist in all of Palestine, and there is only
evidence of campsite and cave occupation. No such campsite layers
have been discovered, but sherds in later contexts indicate that
some of the nonurban folk did camp at Taanach near the beginning
of the 2nd millennium B.C. Taanach entered another period of
prosperity and prominence in the Hyksos period of the 17th and
16th centuries B.C. It had the massive fortifications typical of
the Hyksos period, the fine patrician's house, and caches of
beautiful artifacts in smaller dwellings, all of which attest its
affluence.

Toward the end of the 16th century, at the end of the Middle
Bronze age, Taanach suffered a substantial destruction, but this
did not prevent it from enjoying one of its most flourishing eras
in the next half-century, as attested by a large Late Bronze I
building complex with an adjacent street with fine cobbled and
plastered surfaces and beautiful Tell el-'Ajjûl and Cypriot White
Slip I wares. This prosperous urban phase seems to have been
brought to an end near the middle of the 15th century B.C., probably during the course of Tuthmosis III's destructive campaign of
1468 B.C.

The subsequent history of Taanach is less illustrious. There
is evidence of less pretentious occupation extending about a half-

century after 1468, and the Akkadian tablets may belong to this period as several scholars suggest.[5] The excavations have produced nothing that can be assigned to the period from the late 15th to the late 14th century B.C., a fact which does not recommend the reading of Taanach as the incomplete place name of Amarna text No. 248. So far there is no evidence that Taanach was occupied in the Amarna age (mid-14th century).[6]

There is only sparse evidence of occupation in the 13th century, but several substantial structures of the 12th century have been unearthed. The 12th century occupation does not seem to have been extensive, for large areas of the southwest quarter of the mound were not built up. This occupation ended in a violent destruction, which it is tempting to associate with the victory celebrated in the Song of Deborah (Judges 5). The ceramic tradition suggests a date of about 1125 B.C. for this destruction. It is followed by a century or more for which we have unearthed no evidence of occupation.

The 10th century B.C. found large areas of Taanach unoccupied, but there were important structures on the mound including the Cultic Structure and a cistern courtyard. The former especially was ruined in a major destruction, the pots suggesting a date about the time of Shishak's destructive campaign of 918 B.C. Thereafter, only bits and pieces of buildings represent the occupation at Taanach in the Iron II period (900-587 B.C.). The Persian period is only slightly better represented with part of a substantial building and quite a number of stone-lined pits scattered throughout the excavations. There were a few scattered Early and Late Hellenistic sherds, only one clearly Roman sherd, and nothing Byzantine. The Roman and Byzantine occupants lived at the base of the tell, especially to the north and east. After a long occupational gap an impressive fortress was constructed on the highest part of the mound possibly late in the Abbasid period, and it was quite probably in use during Crusader times. Thereafter the site seems to have been abandoned.

This picture requires revision of commonly held views about the occupation of Taanach. The first is Albright's view (recently revised) that Megiddo and Taanach "were too close to flourish at the same time except very briefly," and so their occupation "tended to be complementary, not simultaneous."[7] Actually, the occupation pattern at Taanach is very similar to that of Megiddo. General prosperity or adversity in the area affected the two sites similarly, and any doubts about the capability of the Esdraelon plain to support towns the size of Megiddo and Taanach five miles apart in periods of prosperity are belied by common prosperity in the Early, Middle, and Late Bronze ages.

This observation applies especially to occupation of the 12th century B.C., both sites apparently suffering a major destruction

about 1125 B.C. followed by an occupational gap. This opposes
Albright's interpretation of "Taanach by the waters of Megiddo"
as making it "practically certain that Megiddo was then in ruins."[8]
It also undermines the traditional argument for assigning the Song
of Deborah to the period between about 1125 and 1075 B.C. when
Megiddo was probably not occupied. The most attractive hypothesis
would seem to associate the victory of Deborah and Barak with the
destruction of these sites about 1125 B.C.--a victory worthy of
this epic song.

Further comparison of Taanach and Megiddo in the Iron age
leads to another warning observation. From the fact that these
neighboring sites were of similar size in the Iron age it might
seem tempting to assume a similar character and population. Such
an assumption would be quite incorrect. Megiddo was crowded with
administrative buildings and probably quite intensively occupied.
The buildings at Taanach were lightly scattered and probably belonged to those who farmed the fertile plain and to their tenants.

The Excavations[9]

As planned by the original staff, the 1963 and 1966 excavators
endeavored to work in four different kinds of material. Fortifications were investigated in the south trench and on the west near
Sellin's West Building to determine the south and west defenses
(see plan, Pl. 19). Nothing remains of the defenses after the
Middle Bronze age, but since Late Bronze and Iron structures
extend as far as the preserved fortification lines it is safe to
assume that the earlier defense walls were repaired or replaced.
The three phases of Middle Bronze fortifications near the West
Building, consisting of the traditional "Hyksos glacis," are
typical of the defenses of the period. On the south three major
phases of the Early Bronze defenses were discovered, employing
scree construction typical of Early Bronze sites. A twelfth
century B.C. building, called the "Drainpipe Structure," with a
well preserved water system and a courtyard with several interesting installations, was also uncovered in the northern part of the
south trench. The courtyard's massive destruction about 1125 B.C.
may perhaps be attributed to the victory celebrated in the Song of
Deborah.

The area chosen in which to seek domestic occupation was less
satisfying: when Late Bronze stratigraphy was finally reached,
instead of a private dwelling on a public street, a public building
on a private street appeared. The cultic area was more rewarding.
The tenth century destruction, which suggested an association with
Shishak's campaign of 918 B.C., contained a mass of material in
two storerooms (Pl. 20): two iron knives over scores of grain jar

sherds; 140 pig astragali (knuckle bones); over eighty mostly reconstructed ceramic vessels (jars, jugs, juglets, pyxides, bowls, cooking pots, lamps, a censer, and an incense stand); fifty-eight well-preserved "loomweights" plus countless fragments of the same, most of them contained in a large crater; blades of seven knives and a sickle and javelin head of iron; four querns, two rubbing stones, and eight stone pestles; four drum-shaped stones and three small stelae; whorls, weights, and beads; an arrowhead, a macehead, a toggle pin, and a complete figurine mold (Pl. 21).

Attempts to unearth public buildings were realized and resulted in one of the most important finds as well as the only significant epigraphic find of the two campaigns. In clearing a thick burned layer in a twelfth century B.C. building, a small Canaanite cuneiform tablet was discovered on the last day of the 1963 campaign. The preservation of the tablet was probably due to the fortunate circumstance that it was baked in the twelfth century destruction fire. While we thought on the day of its discovery that it was a late example of what is traditionally called Ugaritic, it took Delbert Hillers several months to make the decipherment which was published with the preliminary report of the 1963 campaign.[10] The decipherment indicates that the tablet was either an invoice accompanying a shipment of grain or flour to Taanach, or a receipt for the same written in Taanach. Hiller's translation is as follows: "(From) Kokaba. Belonging to p˹ . . . 8 kprt-measures, sifted flour."[11] The tablet provides the first clear indication that this script was used in common business transactions in Palestine, indeed that this script had ever been written in Palestine at all. This vindicates the preference of W. F. Albright to call the script Canaanite cuneiform rather than the traditional, but geographically provincial designation, Ugaritic.

Highlights among the Finds

The Cultic Structure Cache. The cache, attributed to Shishak's destruction, was found in two rooms at the northwest corner of a building which was otherwise not preserved for our excavation (Pl. 20). It is also possible that the incense stand found by Sellin in this area belonged to the same destruction cache. If these associations are correct, it seems preferable to envision an entire building devoted to cult rather than a few rooms with stored cult material in an otherwise secular building. In any case, there is no indication from the architectural remains of anything cultic. The cultic attribution is based on unambiguous cultic artifacts, mixed, to be sure, with ambiguous and common secular material.

The pig astragali are cultic, not merely a group of gaming pieces. Astragali have a long history of cultic use. From the Middle Bronze II period comes a hoard of 70 sheep astragali from a Megiddo tomb, and a contemporary Megiddo tomb contained an astragalus model.[12] They were still used as amulets in the Hellenistic period.[13] Pig astragali must have had a special significance, because these bones are virtually the only pig remains found in the two campaigns. There is good evidence that the pig was used cultically in Palestine; Père de Vaux has even unearthed an underground pig sanctuary at Tell el-Far'ah (north).[14] If there could be any doubt about their cultic context at Taanach, the discovery of a much larger group from a similar and contemporary cult context at Megiddo should be reassuring.[15]

Their precise cultic function remains a matter of speculation. A few of those from Taanach and Megiddo were pierced with one, two, or three circular bores. A few others had been attached to bronze or iron rods. These might be considered evidence in favor of their use in divination and the casting of lots. There is evidence of their use as amulets, however, and the two functions are not mutually exclusive. As amulets they may have been considered charms against the underworld and its evils--if classical relations mean anything. It is also interesting to think of the Old Testament laws about the pig. Is it not much more likely that the pig's uncleanness was associated with its cultic function rather than the common modernizing interpretation that proscription was related to hygenic considerations?

A second group of indisputable cultic objects are the stelae or masseboth. The stela found in the cultic basin has been discussed above. Three additional small stelae were found in the Room 1 destruction. These are more ovoid in shape with flattened bottoms. With this group were found four stone drums some ten cm. thick and just over twenty cm. in diameter. Their context suggests a cultic function. E. R. Goodenough's "round objects" immediately come to mind, though no evidence bearing directly on their function has yet been forthcoming.

Another object which points to the cultic nature of the building is the figurine mold illustrated with a figurine cast from it in Plate 21. Such a complete mold is an extremely rare find for Palestine. It belongs to the tradition of figurines holding a round object over the left breast. Examples of this type are attested in Palestine from the 11th to the 8th century B.C. In some of these parallels the round object is clearly a tambourine, and in view of other clear and contemporary Mesopotamian parallels any attempt to see in this object anything else is probably misguided.[16] The figurine seems to be pregnant, emphasizing the basic fertility associations. The wrist and ankle bands are characteristic of these

figurines. This particular mold may have been responsible for
the only closely parallel figurine, found in a "maṣṣebah room"
at Megiddo--a similar and probably contemporary context. In
contrast to the more common Astarte types, this figurine is
usually found in cultic contexts.[17] The mold seems to be clear
evidence that such figurines were produced in the Cultic Structure.

Other objects which may have been specifically used in the
cult are the censer, the incense stand, the iron cutlery, and the
"loomweights". The censer, called a strainer after the first campaign, is a small, somewhat globular pot with a vertical neck and
tripod base. It has three rows of pierced holes around the
shoulder. The position of the holes does not recommend it as a
strainer, and a case has been made for its use as a censer,[18] a
use certainly befitting the Taanach context. The two square holes
in the stand indicate that it was not a simple functional stand,
and its context, as well as that of parallel material from a contemporary cult context at Megiddo, recommend it as an incense
stand.[19] That the iron knives belong specifically to a cultic
context is suggested by their presence in a Megiddo context with
a stela and a figurine head like that produced by the mold from
our destruction.[20] Iron was still a rather precious commodity
in the late 10th century, and the utility of cutlery in circum-
cision and sacrifice is obvious.

The preliminary report on the 1963 campaign was skeptical
about the large group of "loomweights" found mostly in a large
crater (Pl. 20).[21] Subsequently, Lois Glock stressed to me the
extreme fragility of these unbaked clay doughnuts. Their
fragility and size do not recommend them as loomweights. Last
summer Kathleen Kenyon mentioned that a hoard of them had been
found in a cultic context in Jerusalem, so that, tentatively, an
enigmatic cultic function may be considered. They are reported
to have been found in functional relation to a loom, but convincing evidence has not been published.

The Pebble-filled Pot. Just south of the preserved Cultic
Structure was a patch of nicely plastered floor. Most of the
walls associated with the floor were subsequently robbed, and
still later an Abbasid pit and Sellin's trench disrupted the
adjacent stratigraphy. Removal of the floor itself produced
early 12th century B.C. pottery, dating the use of the floor to
that century. On this floor sat a small cooking pot partly cut
away by a later stratum but well enough preserved to contain a
large group of pebbles. When we began to look through the pebbles
it seemed that this would prove to be another of the enigmatic
stone-filled pots occasionally found in Palestinian excavations,
but it soon became apparent that the pot contained an interesting
group of objects.

Some of the objects were: a conical stamp seal containing an ibex with nursing baby and a scorpion, a scarab with a man raising a stick toward two superimposed animals, three animals of a hard metal--a baboon, a turtle, and a frog, hematite and heavy metal weights--the same shapes in metal and stone, curious shell sticks, a few heterogeneous beads, a rectangular agate block, an iron nail, polishing stones, and numerous pebbles.

This is an intriguing assemblage of objects. That the combination is not mere happenstance is proved by a parallel group of objects from Megiddo.[22] These come from Chamber B of Shaft Tomb 912 and should probably be assigned to its reuse in the Late Bronze II period. Here is a very similar group of heavy metal and hematite weights accompanied by the same kinds of shell sticks. There are also metal animals, in this case probably sheep and cow. To whom should such a group of objects be attributed? A weight-maker, a jeweler, or even a magician might be suggested, but we are merely guessing.

Figurines. Some 83 figurines have been registered during the first two seasons at Taanach. Well over half of these are of the type dubbed by Sellin the "Astarte of Taanach". This type of nude female figurine with hands under breasts seems to range in date at Taanach from the 15th to the 12th century B.C.[23] Another well-known type of nude goddess with long and frequently pierced ears is represented by several examples from the 15th century B.C. There are also a number of Bes figurines from near the beginning of the Iron are.

To whom did these figurines or the figurine mold belong? The answer to this question can perhaps provide a sobering final note. We do know that these figurines and all the other finds were used by the people of Taanach, and we can be fairly precise about when each of them were used. The campaigns have shed considerable light about what was going on at Taanach during the course of its history. Yet there is still a curtain drawn between this and human history. Practically none of the material such as the figurines can be assigned to a particular historical group-- and such groups are the actual bearers of history. We do not know whether the "Astarte of Taanach" was used by one or several or all of the population elements of Late Bronze Taanach. In fact, we do not know the composition of Taanach's population at any period. What was the composition of the town of Taanach when Solomon took administrative control, when Shishak destroyed it? Who was in charge of the Cultic Structure, and who used it? It would certainly be interesting for the biblical historian to know whether Israelites were involved in organizing or practicing this cult. Such questions Palestinian archaeologists, with their plaguing lack of inscriptions, are almost never able to answer satisfactorily.

Postscript: The 1968 Excavations at Taanach.[24]

The third campaign of the joint Concordia-American School
of Oriental Research excavation at Taanach was conducted between
the 4th of June and 19th of August, 1968, with a professional
staff of 34, a technical staff of 15, and a labor force averaging
185. Excavation continued in areas where previous campaigns had
removed Iron age and subsequent occupation, along with a major
extension of the excavation area on the southwest slope and
another small trench across the western defenses. In general the
Bronze age layers produced more interesting structures and richer
finds than those of the Iron age. Only a few of the excavation
highlights are summarized here.

Excavations of the south slope revealed additional detail
about four phases of Early Bronze defenses. All these phases
belong to the middle of the Early Bronze age, from after the
beginning of Early Bronze II to before the end of Early Bronze III.
Khirbet Kerak ware was associated with only the last two phases.
While the crucial evidence is largely obliterated, it seems that
the earliest defense wall at Taanach, constructed on bedrock, had
a sharp corner at the SW corner of the mound. In the second phase
this was replaced by a rounded defense wall. In the third phase
fill for a roadway along and outside the second wall was contained
by a major revetment. In the final phase a massive buttress
strengthened this weak spot in Taanach's Early Bronze defenses.

The only evidence of Middle Bronze II B occupation uncovered
thus far is from mixed fills and apparently belongs to a small
group of squatters, and it is doubtful that more substantial
Middle Bronze II B occupation occurs elsewhere on the mound. Early
in Middle Bronze II C carefully planned leveling and construction
took place within the Early Bronze defenses: a street was formed
with what may be called an insula on each side.

The earlier Middle Bronze II C phase was considerably destroyed
by later construction creating a casemate defense system. Previous
seasons produced evidence of a massive destruction at the end of
Middle Bronze II C. Similar evidence emerged in 1968, but more
striking was the fact that some of the structures survived the
destruction in usable form and were soon renovated and improved.
The "Late Bronze I Building" of the previous seasons turned out to
be such a renovation of the insula between the casemate and the
street, which continued in use in Late Bronze I. The subsidiary
buildings just south of the West Building seem to have been in use
without interruption during the Middle Bronze II C--Late Bronze I
transitional period.

With the two Middle Bronze II C phases were excavated 56 sub-
floor burials, revealing a great variety of intramural burial
practice during the latter part of the Middle Bronze age. Infants

were buried in cysts in the center of the room or adjacent to a wall frequently in a burial jar. Children were buried singly or in pairs in plain or stone-lined cysts. Adults were also buried in stone-lined cysts. There are also clear examples of round shaft tombs with small dome-shaped chambers for child and adult burials. These tombs contained over 130 ceramic tomb-gifts, and other more precious finds were not rare. In the richest burial of an adult grave-goods included two gold earrings and a silver finger ring, a silver toggle pin, and a string of beads of various semi-precious stones. The ring had been worn on the fourth finger of the left hand.

Further excavation on the southern terrace revealed the context of the large groups of Late Bronze I pottery vessels discovered in previous seasons. The latest groups of vessels were sealed by large segments of bedrock. These had apparently been toppled by an earthquake which brought an end to the troglodyte occupation. It seems probable that this Late Bronze I terrace occupation extended over much of the southern terrace of the mound, suggesting a rather large population for Taanach at that time.

The prize find of the season came from the Cult Area. Here a large hoard of objects, some of them cultic, had been discovered in 1963 in a destruction level attributed to the campaign of Shishak in 918 B.C. As excavation in this area penetrated below Iron I to Late Bronze layers, it continued to produce most of the excavation's fragments of fertility figurines and even another hoard of pig astragali in a Late Bronze I context. From the same context came a fragment of a cultic mask. This area had originally been chosen for excavation because it was the find spot of Sellin's famous incense altar. In 1968 a cistern shaft was discovered, which Sellin had located 5 meters south of the main find spot for fragments of his altar. As the shaft area was cleared, great masses of bedrock were found to have collapsed onto the silt layer of the cistern. When these were removed fragments of a cultic stand, very similar to Sellin's but much better preserved, came to light (Pl. 22). The pottery in its immediate context belonged to the horizon of the Shishak destruction.

The stand is a hollowed square over 50 cm. tall of poorly fired clay. The base is open, but the top is capped by a shallow basin. Beneath this at the front are four registers in high relief. At the sides in the lower three registers are reliefs of the bodies of the pairs of figures whose faces project on the front of the stand. Each side of the topmost register bears the complete relief of a winged beast. The back of the stand is plain except for holes, which are also frequent on the sides and front, especially between the legs and under the necks of the beasts. The lowest register has a nude Astarte type grasping at the ears

of flanking lions. The second consists of a pair of winged
sphinxes. Their female appearance and hair suggest their
identification as cherubim. In the third register from the
bottom the traditional scene of two goats eating from a
stylized tree of life is flanked by a second and similar pair
of lions. This motif is virtually identical with that appearing on the lowest register of Sellin's Räucheraltar. In the
center of the top register stands a young bovine surmounted
by a winged sun disc and flanked by what is apparently a pair
of voluted columns.

Whatever the stand's cultic relation, its function does
not appear to have been that of an incense stand, since there
are no traces of incense or burning from its period of use.
In fact, the holes are probably to be considered vestiges of
the windows of earlier "house stands". It may be considered a
cultic stand, probably used for libations.

Chapter X

THE CEMETERY AT BÂB EDH-DHRÂ'

The First Campaign.[1]

In 1958 a trickle of Early Bronze pots began to appear in
Jerusalem antiquities shops. The pots appeared to range from
Early Bronze I to Early Bronze IV, that is, they spanned the
entire Early Bronze period from the latter part of the fourth
to near the end of the third millennium B.C. They were reported
to have come from the Hebron area and even from Qumrân. From
1960 to 1965 the trickle became a stream, then a flood.

Early in 1964 it became clear that at least a major source
for the pots was a cemetery just south of the large fortified
site at Bâb edh-Dhrâ', near the eastern shore of the Dead Sea
facing the Lisan. On 26 October 1964 Siegfried Mittmann, Fellow
of the German Institute, and the writer went to investigate the
area. The report was indeed confirmed, and we returned with some
sixty more or less complete pots, taken from the surface where
they had been carelessly strewn. We were impressed with the
amount of pottery and especially with the vast area where shallow
probings had produced tomb-gifts.

Upon our return we informed colleagues of our findings and
of the need for at least a small expedition to excavate a few of
the tombs scientifically. When it became clear that no other
group was in a position to undertake an early expedition, a small
two-week tomb clearance was planned to begin on 1 March 1965.

It was not difficult to secure a staff for this adventure.
Annual Professor E. F. Campbell, Jr., Fellow Bruce Dahlberg, and
the writer from the American School were joined by Director Martin
Noth and Fellow Siegfried Mittmann of the German Evangelical
Institute for Archaeology in the Holy Land. It was a distinct
pleasure and privilege to have the participation of our German
colleagues in this project, and special thanks are due to the
Institute for supplying the expedition with a second vehicle.
These were assisted in supervising excavation by Mr. Ronald Douglas
of Heidelberg University. In addition, Fouad Zoghbi of Bethlehem
served as draftsman and prepared most of the detailed tomb and
building plans. Muhammed S. Kemal served as surveyor and prepared
the cemetery plan. Miss Renee Lund of Uppsala University aided in
registration. Ibrahim Tarawneh of Kerak represented the Department
of Antiquities. The backbone of the staff was provided by our
veteran Arab staff members Aboud Dhib Nasif, driver and supervisor;
Muhammed Adawi, cook; and Nasir Dhiab, Jaber Muhammed Hussein, 'Abd
er-Rahman Hussein, and Muhammed Ibrahim Hussein, technical diggers.

On 13 March a large truck left the School with our gear at
5:30 a.m. and we left at 6:45 a.m., taking the Mojib road to
Kerak and the fairly good road from Kerak to Ghôr el-Mêzra' at
the edge of the Lisan. We set up camp on an unused roadbed at
the point where the new road turns south for Ghôr es-Sâfi. The
time seemed short, but our hard-working staff finished the job
so quickly that by 6 p.m., when the local military commander
arrived, we were able to relax over a cup of tea and enjoy a view
out over the Dead Sea at dusk.

The usual beginning-of-dig problems were quickly settled.
There was an ample supply of workmen in a neighboring encampment;
there was a good spring for our water supply a few kilometers off;
the cemetery was on government land. Our chief problem was to
locate tombs as efficiently as possible. We made arrangements
for the services of a local expert for the next day and hoped for
the best.

In the morning we hired thirty-five men, eight for each of
four supervisors, a guard, a camp boy, and a water man. The
supervisors divided their men into two four-man search teams, and
we began to probe. Most of the probes on the first day produced
quantities of sherds from several strata. Two things became
apparent: we were digging in a quarter of an apparently large
campsite on the southern slope below the fortified site, and our
expert was trying to lead us away from the cemetery. Dr. Mittmann's
probe, just beyond the confines of the camping area, almost
immediately struck a mudbrick wall a few centimeters below the
surface. This proved to belong to the largest of our charnel
houses, and Dr. Mittmann was occupied for the entire campaign
clearing this building of fallen mudbrick and piles of hundreds
of bones and pots on its cobbled floor.

That evening we had a session with another local expert. His
story fitted perfectly with the first appearance of the pots in
Jerusalem in 1958, but it was only at the end of the dig that the
truth of his story about tombs which produced a truckload of
pottery became credible. The next morning he did his best to help
us locate tombs. His formula was simple: find large smooth black
stones with faces emerging at the surface. His formula worked well
enough though we soon discovered that it was not entirely sound.
Three well-embedded smooth black stones in one place convinced us
that we should dig where we found the shaft of Tomb A 69; on the
other hand, black surface stones at the surface of A 65 proved to
be part of a cairn which was piled over an articulated burial;
elsewhere somewhat smaller black stones proved to be part of the
pavement of one of the charnel houses. The truth was that the
cemetery had been so intensely used that we were almost bound to
hit something wherever we dug. We estimated that if the rest of

the cemetery was as intensely used as the area we worked, it would have contained a minimum of 20,000 shaft tombs!

By the third day of the clearance we already had enough shaft-tombs and funerary buildings to more than occupy us for the projected two-week campaign. The great amount of time to extricate the contents of the buildings from the extreme hard pack of fallen mudbrick which covered them and the desire to find other types of tombs made us decide that the campaign should be extended. We did find three completely undisturbed sealed chambers, but our efforts to find an undisturbed stone-lined, slab-covered tomb merely led to other funerary buildings and shaft tombs. During the last half of the campaign we had to exercise a rigid discipline to keep from starting new tombs or buildings which could not be finished. Even with this effort, the night before our departure saw us like a band of tomb robbers removing 347 pots from just inside the doorway of a new funerary building, which we then left unexcavated.

Bâb edh-Dhrâ' was discovered in 1924 on an expedition to the southeastern Dead Sea basin led by W. F. Albright. Twenty years later he found time to publish a short article on some of the sherds he had collected from in and around the fortress and from a cairn burial.[2] His chronological conclusion was that "the latest possible date for any Bâb edh-Dhrâ' pottery is thus the 21st century B.C., and its maximum scope is 23rd-21st century B.C. I am inclined, moreover, to date most of it about the 22nd century B.C." With this dating I am in complete agreement and would further suggest that the larger pieces which presumably came from the cairn burial[3] should be assigned to the 21st century while the rest of the material associated with the fortress indicates its final use in the 22nd century.

. . . . .

The most exciting archaeological experience to date for the writer was the removal of a blocking stone from the first perfectly sealed chamber we discovered. Despite dislocation by roof fall and silting we were fairly sure of the original tomb plans, but here was a chamber with each pot and bone just as it had been left over forty-five hundred years ago. The serrated marks of the flint tool with which the chamber had been cut were preserved over the entire domed surface. The lines of the mat on which the bone pile was laid were clear, and beneath were cracks in the floor which had dried out before the mat was laid. The twenty-five pots were neatly stacked and nested and it was clear that they had never contained food or liquid; in fact, they had never been used, and most of them did not even need dusting. There was a neat line of skulls: three adults, one child, and one infant. The long bones of adults and the children were carefully placed atop the bone pile.

It will take long hours of pouring over the some two thousand complete pots and hundreds of other complete forms plus detailed tracing of the parallels to the other objects from the cemetery. A campaign with work in the city is certainly indicated. The first impression I have as the "pouring over" process begins is of the tremendous skill of our staff, which accomplished their task with almost no "fresh breaks"--and of the people who made such strong pots. The people that produced a three-million-pot cemetery were as much slaves to pots as archaeologists!

Summary of the Tomb Types after Three Campaigns. [4]

The vast cemetery of Bâb edh-Dhrâ' lay east, west, and south-west of the town occupation. By actual investigation it is over a kilometer long and half that wide, but if additional territory under military restriction is investigated, it will undoubtedly prove considerably larger. More incredible than its size is the intensity of its use. Widely scattered excavations have shown that large areas of the cemetery were used successively four times for burials, and there is considerable stratigraphic evidence for establishing burial sequence. In the first and third phases, the intensity of use staggers the imagination. The shaft tombs of the first phase were laid out in rather regular lines so that no space would be wasted, and in one excavation area the charnel houses of the third phases were built much more closely together than modern village huts. In each of these phases present estimates of the size of the cemetery indicate over half a million burials.

The cemetery has a much larger history than the town. The third phase of cemetery use belongs to the period of the Early Bronze town; the first two preceded and the fourth succeeded it. I have roughly estimated that the initial use of the cemetery occurred in the 32nd century B.C., and its final burials are just over a millennium later.[5] It seems clear that there was no period of disuse throughout this time.

The earliest phase of the cemetery may be roughly assigned to the last century and a half of the fourth millennium B.C. with a slight extension possible in both directions. With one possible exception, all tombs of this phase were shaft tombs cut into soft limestone. The shafts were usually cylindrical, but two of them were beautifully rectangular with rounded corners. They frequently approached a metre in diameter, and most of them were originally from 1.5 to 2.5 metres deep. At the shaft base were small openings to from one to five usually dome-shaped chambers (see Pl. 23). Entrances were covered by slabs, sometimes dressed to size, and plastered against the opening. The shaft was then tightly packed with the excavated lime earth, unless, it seems, there was intention of reusing the shaft for an additional chamber.

A few of the fifty chambers excavated had low, flat roofs, but the rest were dome-shaped. The contents were quite uniform, but nearly every chamber had some unique feature. The chambers averaged some 2.5 metres in diameter and approached a metre in height. In the centre laid on a rush mat, was a pile of disarticulated bones (see Pl. 24); frequently the long bones were laid parallel covering the pile. Invariably to the left of the bone pile (looking from the entrance) was a line of skulls or skull fragments (Pl. 24). Around the walls were placed a number of ceramic vessels, frequently stacked (Pl. 25). In addition, the gifts often included a basalt cup (Pl. 24), sometimes imitated in pottery, or a basalt, limestone or alabaster macehead. Occasionally preserved were wooden staffs (Pl. 24), basketry, and a pair of sandals. Most striking were the seven figurines found in three of the bone piles. They were of a hook-nosed, pierced-ear fertility type, well-known from later in the Bronze age in Palestine.

The lines of skulls included a range from infants to aged. Four to six skulls, on an average, formed the line, and most of the time the long bones corresponded to the number of individuals represented by skulls. At times the catalogue of long bones was incomplete. All the skulls preserved are of the Proto-Mediterranean type, as indeed are all skulls so far recovered from the Bâb edh-Dhrâ' cemetery. Professional examination of some of the perfectly preserved long bones gave no indication that the bones had been previously exposed or buried. A natural interpretation is that these bones were decarnated by cooking.

The pots consisted mostly of small juglets, tiny bowls, and unusually large deep bowls, which seem to be unique in Palestine. None of the pots from the early chambers are decorated with paint, but many of them are red-burnished, some finished to a high polish. The pots are handmade, but the quality of the work in some tomb groups is quite exquisite with very carefully made, thin-walled vessels with highly polished surface frequently decorated by incised bands near the rim.

The second phase is not well represented in our excavations. It involves the introduction of new burial practices and painted decoration on pottery. A single chamber has a single vessel painted in the poor tradition best known from tombs at Jericho, called Proto-Urban A by Kenyon. The striking fact is that in this chamber, for the first time, we encounter a burial practice that is normal in the Early Bronze age. Complete bodies are buried in the shaft tomb chambers, but they were pushed aside when subsequent burials were made in the same chamber. In our chamber four adults were laid in parallel fashion just inside the entry, and bones of previously buried bodies were pushed aside. As this phase progressed the tradition of painting pots improved and new forms were introduced. This improved tradition is called Proto-Urban B at Jericho. Three tombs of the Proto-Urban tradition have been discovered.

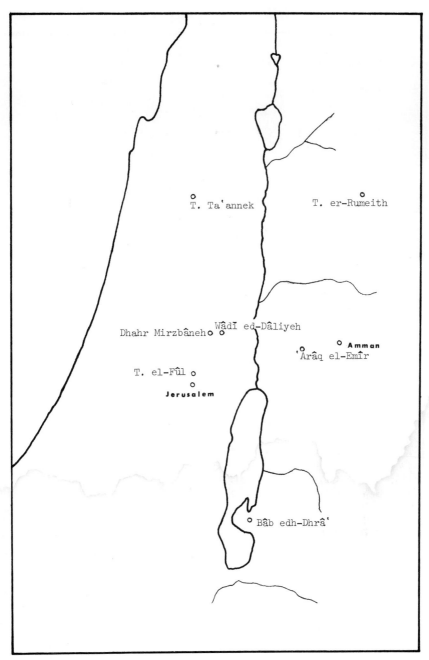

1 Map locating seven sites excavated by Paul W. Lapp.

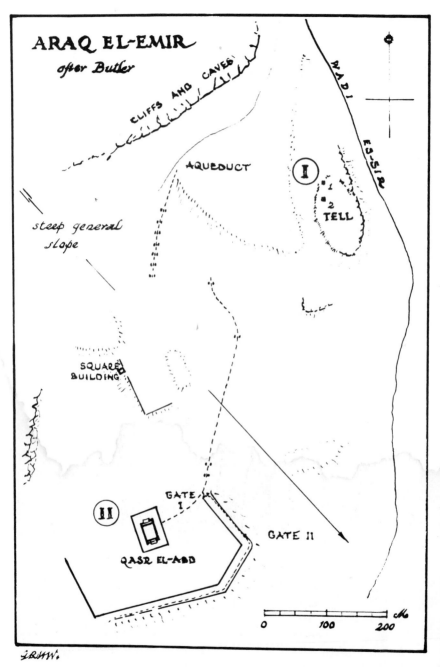

2　Plan of the environs of ʻArâq el-Emîr showing two excavation fields.

3 'Arâq el-Emîr feline sculptured on mottled red and
   white dolomite block inserted in lowest course of
   the Qasr el-'Abd east wall toward north end. Note
   crude insertion, drain in front of animal's right
   forepaw, and remains of Byzantine wall, which protected sculpture, at extreme right. Sculptured
   block moistened for photography.

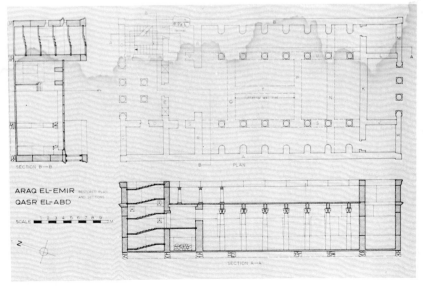

4 Restored plan and sections of the Qasr el-'Abd.

5 Looking northeast at the Plaster Building at Arâq el-Emîr. The south corridor is in the foreground. Meter stick is on the inner wall in which finely dressed blocks flank doorways.

6   Looking east down the Wâdī ed-Dâliyeh to the Jordan
     Valley.

7   Père R. de Vaux of the École Biblique and Yusef Saad
     of the Palestine Archaeological Museum about to
     enter the Wâdī ed-Dâliyeh manuscript cave for the
     first time.

8 Plan of Mugharet Abu Shinjeh,
  the manuscript cave of the
  Wâdî ed-Dâliyeh.

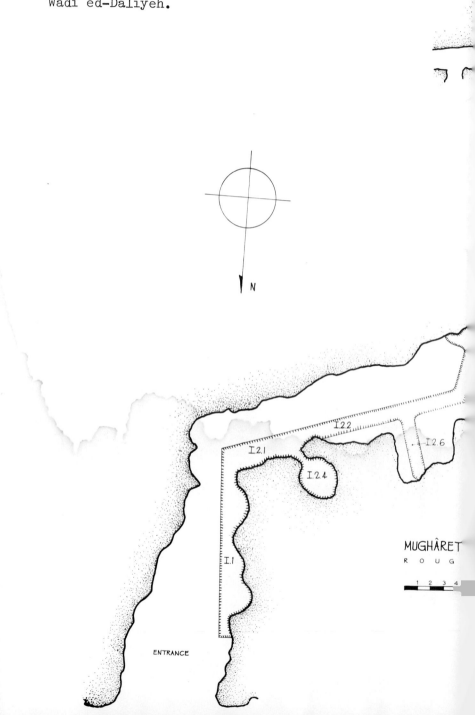

NEW

I.2.2

I.2.1

I.2.4

I.2.6

I.1

ENTRANCE

MUGHÂRET

R O U G

1 2 3 4

N

I.3
MANUSCRIPT
FIND

I2.7

DUMP

I.8

I.5

BAT DOME

I.6

I.7

:HINJEH
: A N

9
M

HOT ROOM

I.4

9 Workers in the manuscript cave carefully examine debris under difficult conditions.

10 Two large Middle Bronze I pots in Cave II of the Wâdî ed-Dâliyeh.

11 Looking south from Cemetery B to Cemetery A and to
Dhahr Mirzbâneh. The laborers in the foreground
are clearing Shafts B 1 and B 2.

12 Shaft of Mirzbâneh Tomb A 4.

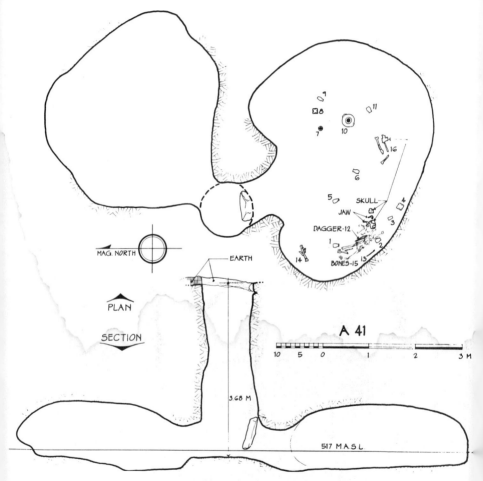

13 Plan and section of Mirzbâneh Tomb A 41.

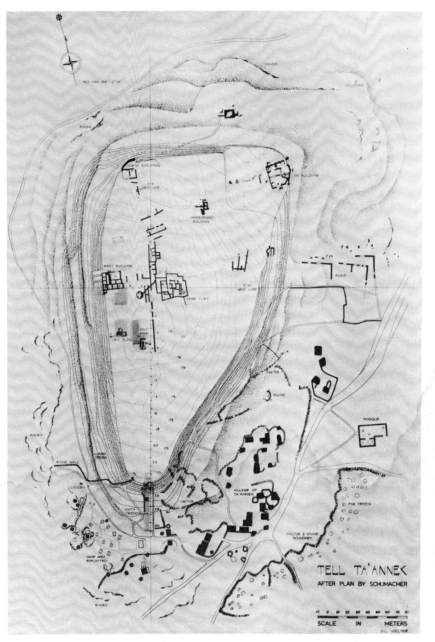

19 Plan of Tell Ta'annek showing German excavations
    with 1963 excavated areas shaded.

20 Storerooms of the cult area from which several hundred artifacts
    came in the 1963 excavations at Taanach.

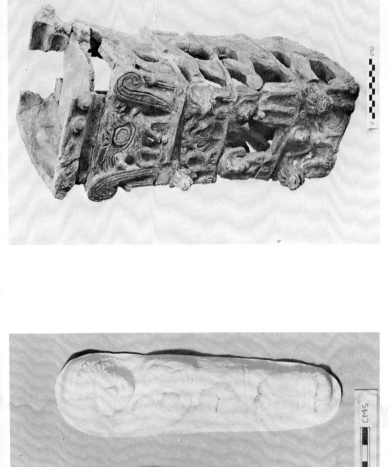

21 The figurine mold from the cultic
    storeroom at Taanach and a
    plaster figurine made from it.

22 Reconstructed cultic stand from
    a tenth century B.C. silt layer
    of a collapsed cistern found at
    Taanach in 1968.

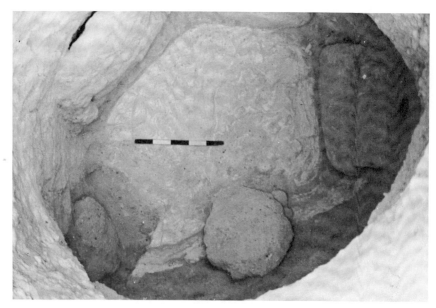

23 Shaft of Tomb A 68 at Bâb edh-Dhrâ' with slabs
blocking five entryways to domed chambers.

24 Bâb edh-Dhrâ' Shaft Tomb A 69 chamber with bone
pile in the center, stone cup and skulls to left,
remains of wooden staff in back center, and bowls
on right.

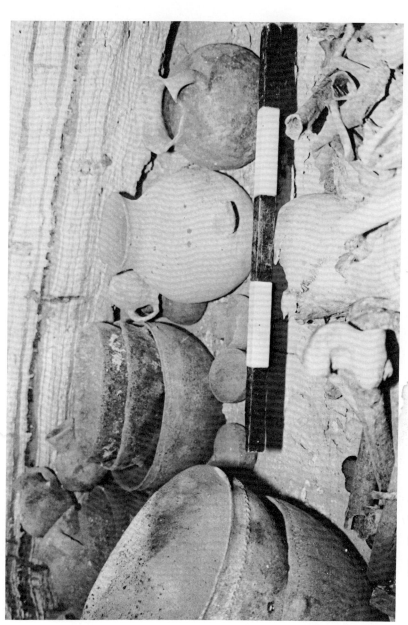

25 Variety of pots and bones stacked in Bâb edh-Dhrâ' Tomb A 72.

26 One of the funerary buildings or charnel houses from the urban period at Bâb edh-Dhrâʿ, the 29th to the 23rd centuries B.C.

27 A tholoi type tomb of the third phase at Bâb edh-Dhrâ'.

28 Looking west as the
1962 spring sound-
ings at Tell er-
Rumeith were in
progress. Four
"squares" were exca-
vated to bedrock:
one on a secondary
knoll to the east
shown in the fore-
ground, one near
the base of the
mound, one on the
steepest part of
the slope where the
fort wall was dis-
covered, and one on
the center top of
the mound (on the
horizon). Eight
strata were defined
and indicated a
larger excavation
would be desirable.

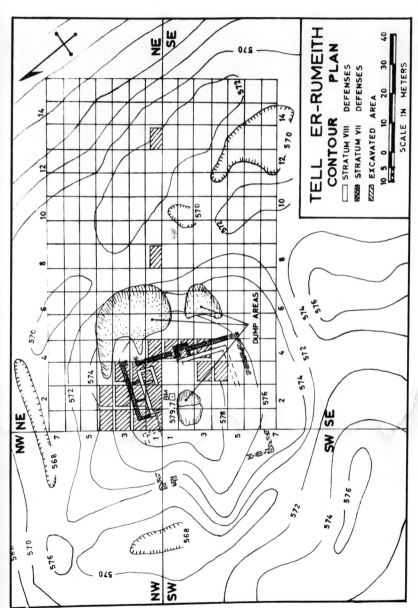

29 Plan of Tell er-Rumeith showing the defenses of Strata VII and VIII.

30 Looking westward at the stone Stratum VII
    defenses with the west gate built against the
    brick Stratum VIII wall (upper left). Note
    the door socket _in situ_ in the entryway
    (center left).

31 Looking eastward at houses of Stratum VI at Tell
    er-Rumeith with a street to the right.

The first was cut into a tomb shaft of the first phase, but
it was badly eroded, and nothing could be determined about the
bones. A second tomb was of the typical shaft-tomb type, but it
had a small slab-lined passage between the shaft and the chamber.
The new feature of the passage persists in all subsequent shaft
tombs so far excavated at Bâb edh-Dhrâ'. The chamber contained
74 pots, a good group of which were beautifully painted in the
Proto-Urban B tradition. The earlier burial tradition persisted,
and there was a pile of disarticulated bones with a skull line to
the left. The third tomb was of a type so far unique at Bâb edh-
Dhrâ'. It was a circular, largely subterranean chamber with walls
of mudbrick and two large slabs flanking its entryway. Its door
was an even larger slab. The chamber was about 5 metres in diameter
and had a second floor or upper shelf on which were deposited
baskets containing bones and pots. There were at least three
articulated burials on the main floor but also heaps of bones pushed
toward the walls. The pots were of the Proto-Urban B tradition,
some beautifully painted.

With the second phase we come to a period with considerable
comparative material from elsewhere in Palestine. That the painted
tradition should not be considered a regional characteristic of
southern Palestine is now quite clear,[6] and Jericho has provided
two tombs with Proto-Urban B remains superimposed on those of Proto-
Urban A. Relations with Egypt make it possible to assign absolute
dates to the phase with some confidence.[7] There is general agreement that the Proto-Urban B period is relatively short. It may be
assigned to the last half of the 30th century B.C. with possible
extension in either direction. The Proto-Urban A phase should be
limited to an even shorter period preceding Proto-Urban B.

The third phase is a long one, extending through the entire
urban period at Bâb edh-Dhrâ', from the 29th to the 23rd century
B.C. The most prominent burial practice throughout this period is
up to now quite unique. It consists of funerary buildings or
charnel houses, rectangular mudbrick buildings from about 3 by 5
to 5 by 7 metres in size (Pl. 26). In plan they do not differ from
the rectangular houses of neighbouring Arad (but without benches)
and elsewhere as well as most of the public buildings and temples
of the Early Bronze age. The best preserved of the eight buildings
excavated, A 51, affords good evidence of the associated burial
practices. Like most of the buildings, it contained piles of disarticulated bones mixed with pots, beads, and occasional copper
weapons. Apparently when the building was considered filled, cloth
was scattered over the bone piles on both floors, a great heap of
bones (mostly skulls) was set on the stairs leading down to the
lower floor from the entryway, the cloth was set ablaze, and the
entryway was sealed by a wall blocking the two brick walls flanking
the slab-lined entryway. This entrance was typically on one of the

broad sides, and no additional openings have been found in any
of the buildings. This building contained bones of over 200
individuals and over 900 complete pots. While unique, the two
stories and the slab-lined entryway point clearly to the Proto-
Urban B round building as the charnel house prototype.

The shaft tomb tradition also continued through the urban
phase, always with the slab-lined entryway first encountered in
Proto-Urban B. Burial practice was invariably that common in
the rest of Palestine, multiple articulated burial followed by
reuse of the chamber with previously buried bones and tomb-gifts
pushed aside. The gifts of pottery provide the same range as the
charnel houses. Of special interest were two such tombs excavated
in the last season which had their shafts filled with medium-sized
stones and contained pots of late Early Bronze III type mixed with
the pots of the succeeding non-urban phase, variously called Early
Bronze IV, Intermediate Early Bronze-Middle Bronze or Intermediate
Bronze age.

Several other kinds of tombs have been discovered in the
cemetery with pottery dating them to the third phase. One is a
tomb entered by stairs leading down to the floor of the dome-
shaped chamber. The chamber walls were lined with small stones,
and all around were small artificial openings, interpreted in
classical tradition as doors for the spirits of the deceased.
Another is a rather rectangular cist large enough for a single
extended burial, which had its walls lined with fairly small stones
and was capped by well-cut flat slabs. Finally, along a line
extending eastward from the ancient town, which presumably represented the ancient road from Kerak to Bâb edh-Dhrâ', was a series
of tholoi some five metres in diameter. In one the lowest course
of large rectangular sandstones, cut to match each other perfectly,
was completely preserved and suggested an originally beehive-shaped
structure (see Pl. 27). Since these were above ground, nothing was
left of their contents except enough potsherds to date them. These
might have belonged to the ruling aristocracy of the town.

Our efforts to learn much about the fourth phase of the cemetery
have been largely frustrated. A number of tomb groups purchased in
the vicinity of Bâb edh-Dhrâ' belong to the post-urban phase and
include the typical unpainted pottery, such as four-spouted lamps
and teapots, and copper daggers. In the excavations we have encountered four cairn burials of this phase, and it is clear that
the stone pile was placed directly upon a single, articulated burial
with legs lightly flexed. In each instance the shallow cist was cut
into a tomb of an earlier phase. These cairn burials are presumably
to be attributed to the destroyers of Early Bronze urban life at Bâb
edh-Dhrâ'. This destruction is linked to the destruction of other
Palestinian, Syrian and Anatolian towns during the course of the
23rd century B.C.

Chapter XI

EXCAVATIONS AT TELL ER-RUMEITH

Jerusalem, July 10, 1967[1]

The winter of 1967 was an unusually cold and wet season in Jerusalem, and it reached its climax in the form of a blizzard on Easter Sunday, March 26. The Rumeith dig was scheduled to get underway on the first day of April, but there was some doubt whether the inclement weather would allow us to comply with our plans. We were fortunate to have some ideal weather right after Easter, so on March 30 the first contingent headed for Rumeith, and on the following day the rest of the staff followed with equal enthusiasm. The 1967 campaign took place between April 1 and May 12, a period of six weeks on a five-day week basis. Out of deference to our Moslem workers we observed the weekly holiday on Friday; out of consideration for the staff Saturday was also included. At the end of the work-day each Thursday the staff wasted no time as they hurried to Jerusalem to re-enter civilization at the American School in the form of a bath and a change of clothes. After being sandblasted for several days each week on the wind-swept mound, the latter were very much in order.

The Rumeith expedition was jointly sponsored by Pittsburgh Theological Seminary and the American Schools of Oriental Research. The budget was provided by the former, and the equipment and transportation by the latter. The staff was composed of the following: Howard M. Jamieson, who represented the Pittsburgh Seminary as co-director and also functioned as treasurer and field supervisor; Susan E. Culp of the University of Pennsylvania, anthropologist and field supervisor; Gavriel Flores, C.SS.R., a Brazilian and student at the École Biblique, field supervisor; also Gustav Jeeninga from Anderson College, Indiana, Edward D. Grohman from Knoxville College, Tennessee, Philip J. King from St. John Seminary, Boston, Robert A. Hutchison from St. Charles, Illinois, and Walter E. Rast from Valparaiso University, Indiana, field supervisors; Thomas Schaub, O.P., from the École Biblique and Aquinas Institute in Dubuque, architect; Fouad Zoghbi of Bethlehem, draftsman; Issa Zoghbi, Bethlehem, assistant draftsman; Aletta Jeeninga of Anderson, registrar; Sister Marie McNamara of Rosary College, River Forest, Illinois, pottery mending; Ahmed Odeh, representative of the Jordan Department of Antiquities. The service staff included Aboud Dhib Nasif as driver and camp manager; Kamel Ikhdayir as cook with two assistants; and Nasir Dhiab as chief technical man with eight assistants from Taanach, Samaria, Balâtah, and Bâb edh-Dhrâ˙. The staff was very dedicated and worked together in a spirit of warm friendship and good humor.

The days and weeks spent at Tell er-Rumeith were busy ones.
The day began shortly after six o'clock when there would be a
great rush to the water storage tank to fill a basin with cold
water for the morning ablutions. Breakfast was served shortly
thereafter, and it consisted of hot cereal, eggs, bread, and
coffee. This was more than adequate preparation for a full day's
work. The workers began to arrive from Ramtha during our breakfast period, which meant that they were well ahead of the seven
o'clock roll-call. The first few hours on the mound were chilly
and windy, but by the time of the coffee break at 9:45, the sun
had warmed the tell to a comfortable degree. The fifteen minute
respite sustained us until noon when work stopped for 45 minutes.
After lunch we excavated for three more hours till 4 o'clock when
the laborers began to return to Ramtha and we fortified ourselves
with tea and bread. Invariably most of the field supervisors then
returned to their plots to draw the top plans or help one another
with section drawings. Darkness would force us to leave the mound
and return to our camp by six o'clock. It was then almost time
for supper. After a half hour elapsed in the mess tent we were
ready to begin the pottery reading. We had worked out a system
so each knew when he was due at the pottery tent, and in that way
there was no delay. The remainder of the evening was given to
preparation of the field books. Pressure lamps are not conducive
to the kind of precision that is required for keeping records so
one has to be careful to double-check each entry. The field book
up to date, it was then almost eleven o'clock and time to retire
for the night. From that moment on no human sound broke the
stillness of the night in the plains of Gilead. Every minute of
sleep counted in order to be ready to face the rigors of the next
day's work.

Our camp consisted of about a dozen tents, mostly of the small
variety, and was located to the east at the base of the mound,
which is largely a rocky outcrop. With the exception of several
chilly nights at the beginning of the season and a strong wind
which cost us a half-day's work, the weather was nearly perfect.
The countryside was green when we began and golden when we finished
--just in time, for we were beginning to lose our workers to the
grain harvest. Despite our pre-Easter apprehensions over the
severe winter rains, it proved to be an ideal time for the campaign. In the end we felt we had a complete enough story of the
tell to abandon the site to some future excavator, and we were
determined to set down the story as soon as possible. However,
the unforeseen event of June has delayed this report.

My last diary notation on the Rumeith dig reads, "The end of
a phase or an era." This was written on May 12, 1967; the first
entry dates back to the sounding of the spring of 1962. I was
thinking of the loss of Aboud, who had always been my right hand

man at excavations, of the talk of major changes for the Jerusalem
School, of the fact that this was the last campaign of a small
scale that I would conduct as part of the School's annual program.
At the time, however, I was not thinking of the Six Day War,
though the final words of my diary were fulfilled like an ancient
prophecy. This accounts for the disjointedness of this letter,
begun in Amman during the war, continued in Tehran and Athens,
and finally finished in Jerusalem. Incidentally let me take this
opportunity to thank all our ASOR friends for their kind expressions
of concern during the crisis, to give assurance that the Lapp
family is safely and happily back home in Shafat, and to express
the hope that some of you will have the opportunity to visit us
during the coming year.

The Stratigraphy

In the course of our six weeks at Tell er-Rumeith we were
pleased to have several visitors. Toward the end of the season
Père Roland de Vaux and Mrs. Crystal Bennett paid us a visit, and
when they finished touring the mound, Mrs. Bennett exclaimed, "An
archaeologist's dream!". The stratigraphy of Rumeith was a model
of simplicity and clarity--none of the usual tossing and turning
in the wee small hours with the nightmare of stratigraphic relation
between fields, or even adjacent squares. Rumeith was a small
fortress, with the east fort wall under 40 meters long. When it
suffered defeat, it was completely destroyed; when it was restored,
the reconstruction was according to an over-all plan.

As the soundings in the spring of 1962 revealed (Pl. 28), the
main stratigraphy of the mound represented an occupation of about
two centuries, ending with Tiglath-pileser's destructive campaign
around 733 B.C. Also discovered in the sounding east of the main
mound was material pertaining to the Hellenistic, Roman, Byzantine
and Arab periods, but this was devoid of substantial architecture
and indicated only transient occupation. Surface sherds, pits,
dugouts for tents, and graves were indicative of the late occupations on the mound proper. In our 1967 campaign excavation was
confined to the fortress itself, so from these late periods (Strata
IV-I) very little was recovered. The large number of burials which
we uncovered in the latest stratum not only surprised us but also
slowed down our work. Artifacts associated with the burials were
very meager.

The chief objective of our 1967 campaign was a further investigation of the four Iron Age strata defined in the 1962 season
(Strata VIII-V). Our purpose this time was to excavate a quarter
or more of the fortress, recover coherent plans of the strata,
and collect ceramic groups in order to add precision to the Syrian

ceramic typology of the period. These objectives were substantially achieved. The northeast quarter of the tell was
excavated either to the earliest stratum or to bedrock, and a
portion of the southeast quadrant along the east fort wall was
also cleared.

While we have been able to confirm the stratigraphic sequence
of the two test-pits we made on the mound in 1962, the correlation
of the layers which we proposed tentatively has proved wrong. The
mudbrick structure founded on bedrock is still to be attributed
to Stratum VIII and the time of Solomon. The stone fort wall,
discovered on the east slope in 1962, continues to be assigned to
Stratum VII and is now seen to be an outer shell added to the
mudbrick fort. The thick-walled stone building near the center
of the fort is not contemporary with the stone fort wall; rather
it is founded on stone debris from the destruction of the fort.
This is reassigned to Stratum VI. The topmost Iron Age stratum
is still designated as Stratum V. The highlights of each stratum
may briefly be described.

Stratum VIII

The seven-meter length of a thin (52 cm.) mudbrick wall
exposed in 1962 turns out to have been a curtain wall, protecting
a recessed gateway with a narrow entrance to the north side. It
adjoins a mudbrick wall 1.25 m. thick, which extends eastward
nearly 15 m. to the northeast corner of the Stratum VIII mudbrick
fort (Pl. 29). The 1.5 m. thick east wall of the brick fort was
almost completely preserved and was founded on a stone socle
resting on bedrock. The south wall located in a small trench was
also 1.5 m. thick. If the fort was symmetrical as contours
suggest, its dimensions were roughly 37 by 32 m. On the basis
of this projection about a fifth of the fort was excavated in
its northeast quadrant.

The room at the northeast corner of the fort had interior
walls virtually as thick as the exterior walls. These form a
room only 3.25 by 2.25 m. The strength of the fortification may
be seen from the fact that the surrounding walls take up nearly
three times as much floorspace as the room itself. Access to the
room was had from the west through a doorway 85 cm. wide with a
well-preserved threshold. The rest of the interior plan we recovered was less regular, and this attests the frequent rebuild-
ings which are normal for such mudbrick structures located in an
area where heavy rainstorms are common.

Unfortunately, work in the vicinity of the entrances to the
fort did not produce clear plans. The presumed gate on the east
side was obliterated by operations connected with the razing of

Stratum VII, and excavation on the area of the north gate was
incomplete. There the thin north curtain wall was recessed 1.75
m. from the main defense line. The stone-lined entrance through
the curtain wall was only 65 cm. wide.

The remains inside the fort were what one would expect to
find in a small settlement located on the barren grain-growing
plateau of Gilead. There was a good repertory of stone grinding
implements, craters, and bowls, all of which attest a well-developed
tradition. It was not unusual to find beehive-shaped ovens in the
rooms, and there were occasional bins set in corners or in the
floor. The amount of ceramic material was surprisingly small, but
it supports the conviction that Stratum VIII pertains to the time
of Solomon. There were a few pockets of debris which preceded
stratigraphically the Stratum VIII fort construction, but these
produced very little. Some rooms revealed two Stratum VIII floors,
each with superimposed burnt destruction debris. The final destruction must have been quite substantial, producing as much as
a half-meter of burnt debris. Wherever bedrock was cleared, there
was increasing evidence of a substantial operation of leveling
bedrock prior to the construction of the fort.

The Aramean Period - Strata VII-VI

Outside the fort there was no evidence from Stratum VIII.
Either the flat bedrock shelf had been kept clean, or, more
probably, it was cleared at the beginning of Stratum VII operations.
Shortly after the destruction of Stratum VIII the occupants of
Stratum VII surrounded the brick fort with an impressive stone
defense line over 1.5 m. thick and composed of very large and
roughly dressed boulders. To the north the 3.25 m. interstice
between the two defense walls was divided into casemates by
thinner stone walls. To the east the 1.75 m. interstice was
divided in the same way (see Pl. 29).

The two gateways of Stratum VIII were reutilized in Stratum
VII. The northern gateway provided the best evidence for the
stratigraphic separation of the two strata, for the foundation
trench of the crosswall situated along the east side of the entry
clearly cut through the debris of the final Stratum VIII destruction. It may be that originally the tiny entrance through the
recessed curtain wall of Stratum VIII was reused, but during the
course of Stratum VII occupation the entrance was obstructed by a
poor stone-wall filling in the north face of the defense line.
The entrance plan is uncertain because the subsequent structures
in the gateway were not removed.

The plan of the east entrance was completely preserved (Pl.
30). The large door socket was still in place, even though it was

shattered in the massive destruction of the Stratum VII defenses.
The entrance itself was only about a meter in width. It was
protected to the south by a guardroom which projected slightly
from the defense line. The outer wall of the guardroom was only
slightly thicker than the defense line itself; the Stratum VIII
brick defense wall served as its inner wall (Pl. 30). The entire
room, some 4 by 3 m., and the gateway were filled with about 2 m.
of destruction debris which included a nice pottery group.

Evidence of the same major destruction was a dominant stratigraphic feature all along the Stratum VII defense line and also in
the rooms of the brick fort, which were reused in Stratum VII.
Perhaps a third of all the excavated debris in the northeast
quadrant of the fort belonged to this destruction. The thick destruction layer remarkably preserved the Stratum VII plan. For
example, the wall on the west side of the north entrance of the
brick fort was preserved to a height of over 2.5 m. from its
original foundation on bedrock; and it had about 2 m. of Stratum
VII destruction against it. The debris along the defense line
consisted mainly of burnt brick which contained many large charred
beams from the fort's superstructure. When we reached the floors
a good group of pots, stone implements, and a few installations
were recovered. While rather disappointing, the finds did provide
a clear contrast with Stratum VIII. The material was not the
typical Palestinian repertory of Stratum VIII, but of quite
distinct Syrian tradition. This dates the massive destruction
to the middle of the ninth century B.C.

One reason for the lack of more spectacular finds might be
thought of in terms of the operations which took place right
after the destruction. Just inside the Stratum VII east gate, in
the area of the Stratum VIII gate, the entire gateway area was
cleared to bedrock; and then the excavated debris was tipped back
into the gateway from the south and north. The most plausible interpretation of this curious phenomenon seems to be that it was an
attempt to retrieve something of value from the destruction debris.

The refilling of the gateway was part of an overall reconstruction of the fort soon after the Stratum VII destruction. The
reconstruction involved the creation of a platform over the thick
burnt layer. On the north side the Stratum VII defense wall was
torn down to platform level, and its smashed boulder fragments
thrown into the rooms where debris had not accumulated to platform
level. On the east the defense line and tower were robbed, and
the destruction debris inside was covered by a poor stone revetment
which prevented its collapse on a lower level of occupation upon
the defense line and east of it.

The platform itself consisted of a thick layer of hard gray
clay. It was apparently laid over the entire area defined by the
Stratum VII fort wall, for it was a consistent stratigraphical

feature wherever we dug. In the northeast quadrant only tatters
of wall foundations remain from the structures erected on the
platform (Stratum VI). Presumably this is because the stone was
reutilized in Stratum V construction.

Fortunately in the southeast quarter of the former fort the
Stratum VI plans were well-preserved. This agrees with the evidence
from the platform's preparation that the construction of Stratum VI
followed a single overall plan which was consistently executed.
Walkways between houses were set out in a rectangular grid and had
similar width and composition (Pl. 31). These houses were alike
in character and plan. The walls were only 50 cm. thick; and the
lower half-meter or more was composed of rough small stones, and
this was capped with mudbrick. The dimensions of the rooms never
exceeded 3.5 m. House units consisted typically of two rooms, one
with a cobbled floor and the other containing the foundations for
a stairway to the roof. Evidence of burnt roof poles with thin
white layers of lime rolled upon them was recovered. The floors
of Stratum VI houses in the southeast quadrant were covered with
a thick burnt layer. Several of the rooms contained significant
ceramic groups, which have been dated about 800 B.C. Except for
further evidence of the well-developed stone-working tradition,
other finds were few and of little interest.

The Last Days of the Town - Stratum V

Strata VI and V expanded the occupied area beyond the fort
lines to the north and east. There was a terracing downward near
the defense line, but the extent of expansion is obscured by the
erosion of the mound, which sliced a steep slope especially to
the north. This has robbed us of any evidence concerning the
defenses of these strata. If they ever existed for the expanded
area of occupation, we found no trace of them.

The Stratum V occupation was substantially preserved wherever
we excavated inside the Stratum VII fort lines. This was the last
architectural stratum of occupation. Its walls were commonly
preserved to a meter and a half in height, and its rooms were
filled with destruction debris and artifacts. In the northeast
quadrant the walkways between houses were virtually identical with
those described in the southeast Stratum VI. In fact, the latter
continued to be resurfaced with alternate layers of gravel and
clay in Stratum V. The northeast constructions were also of the
same sort--thin walls with small-stone lower walls capped by mudbrick. The houses in the southeast were reused in Stratum V after
a thick fill raised their floors, and the extant houses were almost
entirely of mudbrick. A final phase of the use of the southeast
Stratum V houses, after the general Stratum V destruction, included

a new feature--mudbrick floors. This occupation ended, apparently
very quickly, with the abandonment of the site, since there is no
evidence of destruction on the brick floors.

One amazingly preserved Stratum V installation in the northeast quadrant deserves special mention. It is a copper-refining
kiln located above and inside the north Stratum VII defense line.
Its brick floor was dotted with flues to conduct heat from the
firebox below. The small basement room from which fuel was fed
into the firebox was also excavated. Here, and elsewhere in the
vicinity of the kiln, large quantities of copper slag were recovered. Most of the kiln's superstructure was eroded away, but
erosion had not completely robbed us of the plan. The kiln is
of the same basic type as those known from earlier and later
periods in Palestine but seems to be a unique example for its time.

After the soundings of 1962 a correlation of the stratigraphic
results with historical events was attempted.[2] Hesitation about
the correlation made me reticent about additional publication.
Subsequently, Gustavus F. Swift kindly supplied me with a copy
of his dissertation on the Iron Age pottery of the 'Amūq.[3] While
chronology is not precise and there are difficulties in view of
the limited amount of published evidence, it seems justified to
conclude that the 'Amūq material generally supports the dating of
the 1962 Rumeith pottery. The excavation of a northern site in
Israel with a similar history[4] is also interesting in this
connection.

The 1967 excavations have nicely confirmed the ceramic
chronology in detail, and Père R. de Vaux has independently
proposed the same dates for groups from Strata VII and V. This
means that the earlier correlations need revision only in detail.
The construction of the Stratum VIII brick fort may continue to
be considered Solomonic and the enclosure a fortified administrative center. Stratum VIII was destroyed near the beginning of the
ninth century B.C., perhaps about 885 B.C. when the area came under
the control of the Arameans. The fort construction of Stratum VII
could be related to the conversion of the site into an Aramean
border fort. Certainly the ceramic evidence for a transfer to
Aramean control in Stratum VII is convincing. The destruction
of Stratum VII in the mid-ninth century may continue to be
attributed to the campaign of Jehoshaphat and Ahab, or of Ahaziah
and Jehoram.

Since evidence for a Stratum VI destruction has been forthcoming, it is possible to suggest that this occupation is to be
attributed to the Arameans from the time Hazael extended the
borders of Syria south of Rumeith (and hence defenses were not
crucial) until the end of the ninth century when Joash defeated
the Arameans at Aphek (and may also be responsible for the Stratum
VI burn). The major destruction of Stratum V may still be assigned

to Tiglath-pileser III's destructive campaign of 733 B.C., and
the subsequent reuse of houses with brick floors might be related
to a stationing of some troops or veterans at the site for a
short period thereafter.

The question of the identification of Tell er-Rumeith with
biblical Ramoth-gilead has not been conclusively proved by the
excavations, but the case is as strong or stronger than for many
biblical sites. The continuity of the name, the congruence of
occupational history with that of the literary record, and its
geographical position fit such an identification. The smallness
of the site is probably the strongest argument against identification. If it is not Ramoth-gilead, it is certainly one of the 60
towns "with walls and bronze bars" controlled by Ben-geber (I Kings
4:13). But this objection must be coupled with evidence for a
larger site in the area with equally impressive claims if it is to
replace Tell er-Rumeith as the most viable candidate for Ramoth-
gilead.

APPENDICES

Appendix I

BIBLIOGRAPHY OF PAUL W. LAPP'S EXCAVATIONS
and State of Final Publication

(For full bibliography of each site through 1970 see "Bibliography
of Holy Land Sites," compiled by E. K. Vogel, Hebrew Union
College Annual, XLII (1971), pp. 1-96.)

'ARÂQ EL-EMÎR

Lapp, P. W. "Soundings at 'Arâq el-Emîr (Jordan)," Bulletin
of the American Schools of Oriental Research, 165 (Feb.,
1962), pp. 16-34.

_____. "The 1961 Excavations at 'Arâq el-Emîr," Annual
of the Department of Antiquities of Jordan, 6-7 (1962),
pp. 80-89.

_____. "The Second and Third Campaigns at 'Arâq el-Emîr,"
Bulletin of the American Schools of Oriental Research,
171 (Oct., 1963), pp. 8-39.

Brett, M. J. B. "The Qasr el-'Abd: A Proposed Reconstruction,"
Bulletin of the American Schools of Oriental Research,
171 (Oct., 1963), pp. 39-45.

Hill, D. K. "The Animal Fountain of 'Arâq el-Emîr," Bulletin
of the American Schools of Oriental Research, 171 (Oct.,
1963), pp. 45-55.

Lapp, P. W. "The 1962 Excavation at 'Arâq el-Emîr," Annual
of the Department of Antiquities of Jordan, 10 (1965),
pp. 37-42.

Considerable preliminary work toward final publication was
done after the campaigns, and N. L. Lapp soon hopes to undertake the editing of the final work.

WÂDÎ ED-DÂLIYEH

Lapp, P. W. "The Samaria Papyrii," Archaeology, 16 (1963),
pp. 204-206.

Cross, F. M. "The Discovery of the Samaria Papyri,"
    Biblical Archaeologist, 26 (1963), pp. 110-121.

Final publication is now in the press and should appear as
Annual of the American Schools of Oriental Research, Vol.
XLI, in 1975.

DHAHR MIRZBÂNEH

Lapp, P. W. The Dhahr Mirzbâneh Tombs (New Haven: American
    Schools of Oriental Research, 1966), x + 116 pp., 44
    figs., and 16 pls.

The above work completed the publication of the tomb excavations.

TELL EL-FÛL

Lapp, P. W. "Tell el-Fûl," Biblical Archaeologist, 28 (1965),
    pp. 2-10.

Final publication now in progress by N. L. Lapp, J. A. Graham,
and H. M. Jamieson.

TA'ANNEK

Lapp, P. W. "The 1963 Excavation at Ta'annek," Bulletin of
    the American Schools of Oriental Research, 173 (Feb.,
    1964), pp. 4-44.

Hillers, D. R. "An Alphabetic Cuneiform Tablet from Taanach
    (TT 433)," Bulletin of the American Schools of Oriental
    Research, 173 (Feb., 1964), pp. 45-50.

Lapp, P. W. "Taanach by the Waters of Megiddo," Biblical
    Archaeologist, 30 (1967), pp. 2-27.

_____. "The 1966 Excavations at Tell Ta'annek," Bulletin
    of the American Schools of Oriental Research, 185 (Feb.,
    1967), pp. 2-39.

_____. "A Ritual Incense Stand from Taanak," Qadmoniot,
    2 (1969), pp. 16-17 (in Hebrew).

_____. "The 1968 Excavations at Tell Ta'annek," Bulletin of the American Schools of Oriental Research, 195 (Oct., 1969), pp. 2-49.

Glock, A. E. "A New Ta'annek Tablet," Bulletin of the American Schools of Oriental Research, 204 (Dec., 1971), pp. 17-30.

The Iron Age Pottery volume by W. E. Rast is at the press. Work on the other volumes continue under the general editorship of A. E. Glock.

BÂB EDH-DHRÂ'

Lapp, P. W. "The Cemetery at Bâb edh-Dhrâ'," Archaeology, 19 (1966), pp. 104-111.

_____. "Bâb edh-Dhrâ', Tomb A76 and Early Bronze I in Palestine," Bulletin of the American Schools of Oriental Research, 189 (Feb., 1968), pp. 12-41.

_____. "Bâb edh-Dhrâ', Perizzites and Emim," in Jerusalem through the Ages (Jerusalem: Israel Exploration Society, 1968), pp. 1-25.

_____. "Palestine in the Early Bronze Age," in Near Eastern Archaeology in the Twentieth Century. Essays in honor of Nelson Glueck, ed. by J. A. Sanders (Garden City, N.Y.: Doubleday & Co., 1970), pp. 101-132.

Schaub, R. T. "An Early Bronze IV Tomb from Bâb edh-Dhrâ'," Bulletin of the American Schools of Oriental Research, 210 (Apr., 1973), pp. 2-19.

The volume on the Early Bronze I pottery by R. T. Schaub and the volume on tomb typology by W. E. Rast near completion and should go to press shortly. Two additional volumes will be prepared by Rast and Schaub with contributions by others.

TELL ER-RUMEITH

Lapp, P. W. "Tell er-Rumeith," Revue Biblique, 70 (1963), pp. 406-411.

_____. "Tell er-Rumeith," _Revue Biblique_, 75 (1968), pp. 98-105.

The Pottery volume is being prepared by J. A. Sauer.

Appendix II

A MEMORIAL MINUTE

The Faculty of Pittsburgh Theological Seminary

Thursday, May 28, 1970

Paul Wilbert Lapp   August 5, 1930-April 26, 1970

When word came of the death of Paul Lapp, Pittsburgh Theological Seminary was stunned. Critical events were taking place
the world over but the sudden termination of a career filled with
rich promise produced a turmoil of emotion which dulled the
thought processes. The response in Pittsburgh was shared in
Jerusalem for the Secretary at the American School of Oriental
Research wrote, "The news fell like thunder and a big black cloud
hovered over us." President Donald G. Miller expressed succinctly
the reaction of many in his memorial address when he said, "The
cadences of our eulogies...(are) but ghastly memoranda placarding
the greatness of our loss."

Paul W. Lapp was born in Sacramento, California on August 5,
1930, the son of Mr. and Mrs. Wilbert H. Lapp. He began his work
for the baccalaureate degree at Concordia College, Oakland, California. The A.B. degree was received in 1951 from Concordia
Theological Seminary, St. Louis, Missouri, and the Diploma in
Theology was granted from the same institution in 1955. Working
on several programs concurrently, he received an M.A. in Education
at Washington University in St. Louis in 1952, and his Ph.D. in
Education from the University of California, Berkeley, in 1955.
Doctoral studies in Semitic Languages and Near Eastern Archaeology
were pursued in the years 1955-57 at Johns Hopkins University.
The year 1957-1958 was devoted to continuing these studies as a
Fellow of the American Schools of Oriental Research in Jerusalem.
In 1958 he returned to the United States and entered Harvard
Divinity School as a candidate for the Th.D. degree. His disser-
tation received the grade of "excellent" and the degree was awarded
in 1960. The American Schools of Oriental Research published the
doctoral dissertation entitled, Palestinian Ceramic Chronology,
200 B.C. to A.D. 70. In 1959 he became a member of the American
University faculty in Washington, D.C.

Paul Lapp's excellence as a Palestinian archaeologist and an
Orientalist began to be noted more widely when he became Annual
Professor of the American School of Oriental Research in Jerusalem
in 1960. Amazingly active, unusually adaptable to the locale,
keenly sensitive to the people of the land and remarkably endowed
with an inquisitive and retentive mind he produced in the period
from 1960-1968 enough research in field archaeology to last a

lifetime. Some would compare those eight years in Jerusalem to
the Albright and Glueck eras of the American School's history.
Among the sites excavated are: 'Arâq el-Emîr, Tell el-Fûl, the
caves of Wâdî ed-Dâliyeh, the necropolis at Bâb edh-Dhrâ', Tell
er-Rumeith and Taanach. At each site something significant was
attempted in field technique and something of value was added to
the knowledge of the history of man in the Near East.

It was in the summer of 1968 that Paul Lapp became a member
of the faculty of Pittsburgh Theological Seminary as Professor of
Old Testament and Archaeology. In a tradition inaugurated in the
nineteen twenties by M. G. Kyle and carried on by James L. Kelso,
Paul Lapp brought to Pittsburgh the vigorous enthusiasm of a
young scholar, the achievement of a world-recognized authority
and the driving ambition of a visionary who saw Palestinian archaeology as but in its early stages so far as excavation methodology
and analytic techniques are concerned.

While it was expected that Paul Lapp would enhance his reputa-
tion as a scholar while at Pittsburgh Seminary with continuing
activity in field archaeology and in writing and publishing, what
came as something of a bonus and a most welcome addition to the
community was a warm interest in theological students as persons
and participation in the total life of the faculty. No student
found that Paul Lapp was unapproachable--rather he willingly spent
hours with groups and individuals because he was concerned for the
total life of all the members of the community. Frequent were the
times when the Dean of Students would be alerted to an individual's
problem as it had come to light in a Twentieth Century A.D. conversation in an office lined with archaeological tomes reporting
on the issues confronting man in the Stone Age or the Bronze.
Faculty committee assignments as diverse as curriculum and worship
were accepted with equal eagerness and each received its fair share
of concern and energy.

Everything he did was achieved by an intensity of concentration
characteristic of but a few. This intensity was united with subject
mastery and as a result over sixty items are listed on his bibliography. However, not as many people knew the other Paul Lapp, the
enthusiastic prankster, the jokester, the one who could heartily
laugh. Perhaps the boyish grin and the often appearing shyness
were clues to this other side of the man. The relaxed Paul Lapp
was frequently seen on a dig after the evening meal. With both
American and Arab staff gathered together, stories would be told,
jokes would be shared, pranks would be played, songs would be sung,
always in English and Arabic, and with Paul Lapp as the personality
bringing all together. Very few knew that he was an accomplished
organist but his love of music was but one clue of a universality
which was unique. It was the ability to closely identify with the
workmen which caused this man to become intensely involved in what

he regarded as a grave injustice inflicted by an indifferent
world upon the Palestinian. As in all things, his political
views were strong and he defended them with vigor. This created
conflict and controversy but no one questioned his integrity,
whether the subject was political or theological, or ecclesiastic
or scholarly.

Paul Lapp was a churchman. He was ordained to the Lutheran
ministry in 1955. In Jerusalem and in Pittsburgh he preached
frequently but when not conducting a service of worship he was
with his family as a faithful and ardent worshiper.

In January of 1970 Professor Lapp visited Morocco, Egypt,
Jordan, Lebanon and Cyprus during a three week tour. In each
country there was an invitation to conduct archaeological research
for at the age of thirty-nine he was known as the most brilliant
Near Eastern field archaeologist of his generation. The published
papers in epigraphy, philology, history and the numerous disciplines
of field archaeology were well known. His leadership was coveted.
The decision was made to join with the State University of New York
at Albany in an initial archaeological effort at Idalion on Cyprus.
In mid-April 1970, after a meeting in New York with those concerned
for the plight of the Palestinians, he went to Holland for a brief
discussion with H. J. Franken on matters of technical analysis.
Paul Lapp had written of Franken, "In matters of technical analysis
Franken's is a voice crying in the desert...It seems quite appro-
priate to suggest that if his voice is heard and his example
followed, the desert would begin to bloom." Paul Lapp heard the
voice and was excited over the prospect of using Franken's techniques
developed at Tell Deir Alla on the Idalion project. However, on
April 26, while swimming with friends from Albany at a popular
beach near Kyrenia, a strong undertow swept Paul out from shore.
He was reached too late to save his life. The exciting prospects
at Idalion disappeared in that moment. Original research of
amazing magnitude awaits publication. Where is the one who is as
rigorously honest and as completely disciplined with the mind as
sharply honed as Paul Lapp, who will comprehend the work done and
continue the intense search for truth?

He is survived by his wife and fellow archaeologist, Nancy Renn
Lapp, and their five children, Deborah, Daniel, Sharon, Diana and
David. His family was the constant joy of his life.

We, the members of the Faculty of Pittsburgh Theological
Seminary, have had taken from our midst an eminent scholar and an
esteemed friend. We would assure Nancy and the children that their
great loss is also ours. We would together acknowledge that we are
richer because Paul was able to give of himself to all of us so
lavishly.

Appendix III

BIBLIOGRAPHY OF PAUL W. LAPP

1958
"A Comparative Study of a Hellenistic Pottery Group from Beth-Zur," Bulletin of the American Schools of Oriental Research, 151 (Oct., 1958), pp. 16-27 (with N. Lapp).

1960
"Late Royal Seals from Judah," Bulletin of the American Schools of Oriental Research, 158 (Apr., 1960), pp. 11-22.

1961
Review of EXCAVATIONS AT JERICHO, VOL. I, by Kathleen Kenyon, American Journal of Archaeology, 65 (1961), pp. 69-70.

Palestinian Ceramic Chronology 200 B.C.-A.D. 70. (New Haven, 1961), x + 231 pp.

1962
"'Arâq el-Emîr" in "Chronique Archéologique," Revue Biblique, 69 (1962), pp. 94-97.

"The 1961 Excavations at 'Arâq el-Emîr," Annual of the Department of Antiquities of Jordan, 6-7 (1962), pp. 80-89.

"Soundings at 'Arâq el-Emîr (Jordan)," Bulletin of the American Schools of Oriental Research, 165 (Feb., 1962), pp. 16-34.

1963
Review of ORIENTAL ART IN ROMAN PALESTINE, by Michael Avi-Yonah, American Journal of Archaeology, 67 (1963), pp. 105-106.

Arabic for the Beginner in Archaeology (Jerusalem, 1963), 63 pp. (with Najua Husseini).

"The Second and Third Campaigns at 'Arâq el-Emîr," Bulletin of the American Schools of Oriental Research, 71 (Oct., 1963), pp. 8-39.

"Tell er-Rumeith" in "Chronique Archéologique," Revue Biblique, 70 (1963), pp. 406-411.

"'Arâq el-Emîr" in "Chronique Archéologique," Revue Biblique,
    70 (1963), pp. 411-416.

"Ptolemaic Stamped Handles from Judah," Bulletin of the American
    Schools of Oriental Research, 172 (Dec., 1963), pp. 22-35.

"Observations on the Pottery of Thâj," Bulletin of the American
    Schools of Oriental Research, 172 (Dec., 1963), pp. 20-21.

Review of L'ARCHEOLOGIA CHRISTIANA IN PALESTINA, by Bellarmino
    Bagatti, American Journal of Archaeology, 67 (1963), p. 434.

"Palestine: Known but Mostly Unknown," Biblical Archaeologist,
    26 (1963), pp. 109-134.

"The Samaria Papyri," Archaeology, 16 (1963), pp. 204-206.

1964
"The 1963 Excavation at Ta'annek," Bulletin of the American
    Schools of Oriental Research, 173 (Feb., 1964), pp. 4-44.

"Tell Ta'annak" in "Chronique Archéologique," Revue Biblique,
    71 (1964), pp. 240-246.

"Tawfiq Canaan in Memoriam," Bulletin of the American Schools
    of Oriental Research, 174 (Apr., 1964), pp. 1-2.

"Report of the Director of the School in Jerusalem" Bulletin of
    the American Schools of Oriental Research, 175 (Oct., 1964),
    pp. 9-11.

1965
"Tell el-Fûl," Biblical Archaeologist, 28 (1965), pp. 2-10.

Review of THE BRONZE AGE CEMETERY AT GIBEON, by James B. Pritchard,
    American Journal of Archaeology, 69 (1965), pp. 180-181.

"The 1962 Excavation at 'Arâq el-Emîr," Annual of the Department
    of Antiquities of Jordan, 10 (1965), pp. 37-42.

Review of STUDIEN ZUR GESCHICHTE ISRAELS IM PERSISCHEN ZEITALTER,
    by Kurt Galling, Journal of Biblical Literature, 84 (1965),
    pp. 297-300.

"Tell el-Fûl" in "Chronique Archéologique," Revue Biblique, 72
    (1965), pp. 394-401.

"Dahr Mirzbâneh" in "Chronique Archéologique," Revue Biblique,
    72 (1965), pp. 401-405.

"Wâdi ed-Dâliyeh" in "Chronique Archéologique," Revue Biblique,
    72 (1965), pp. 405-409.

1966
"The Cemetery at Bâb edh-Dhrâ', Jordan," Archaeology, 19
    (1966), pp. 104-111.

The Dhahr Mirzbâneh Tombs (New Haven, 1966), x + 116 pp., 44
    figs., and 16 pls.

"Bâb edh-Dhrâ'" in "Chronique Archéologique," Revue Biblique,
    73 (1966), pp. 556-561.

"Report of the Director of the School in Jerusalem (1963-1964),"
    Bulletin of the American Schools of Oriental Research, 181
    (Feb., 1966), pp. 10-11.

"Report of the Director of the School in Jerusalem (1964-1965),"
    Bulletin of the American Schools of Oriental Research, 181
    (Feb., 1966), pp. 12-13.

1967
"Taanach by the Waters of Megiddo," Biblical Archaeologist,
    30 (1967), pp. 2-27.

"The 1966 Excavations at Tell Ta'annek," Bulletin of the American
    Schools of Oriental Research, 185 (Feb., 1967), pp. 2-39.

"The Conquest of Palestine in the Light of Archaeology," Concordia
    Theological Monthly, 38 (1967), pp. 283-300.

"The Cemetery at Bâb edh-Dhrâ', Jordan," in Archaeological Dis-
    coveries in the Holy Land (New York: Archaeological Insti-
    tute of America, 1967), pp. 35-40.

1968
Review of EXCAVATIONS AT JERICHO, VOL. II, by Kathleen Kenyon,
    American Journal of Archaeology, 72 (1968), pp. 77-79.

"Bâb edh-Dhrâ'" in "Chronique Archéologique," Revue Biblique,
    75 (1968), pp. 86-93.

"Tell Ta'annak" in "Chronique Archéologique," Revue Biblique, 75 (1968), pp. 93-98.

"Tell er-Rumeith" in "Chronique Archéologique," Revue Biblique, 75 (1968), pp. 98-105.

"Editorial Foreword" to Ovid R. Sellers, et al., "The 1957 Excavation at Beth-zur," Annual of the American Schools of Oriental Research, 38 (1968), p. iii.

"The Excavation of Field II" in Ovid R. Sellers, et al., "The 1957 Excavation at Beth-zur," Annual of the American Schools of Oriental Research, 38 (1968), pp. 26-34.

"Iron II--Hellenistic Pottery Groups" in Ovid R. Sellers, et al., "The 1957 Excavation at Beth-zur," Annual of the American Schools of Oriental Research, 38 (1968), pp. 54-79 (with N. Lapp).

"Bâb edh-Dhrâ' Tomb A76 and Early Bronze I in Palestine," Bulletin of the American Schools of Oriental Research, 189 (Feb., 1968), pp. 12-41.

"If a Man Die, Shall He Live Again?" Perspective, 9 (1968), pp. 139-156.

Review of WINERY, DEFENSES, AND SOUNDINGS AT GIBEON, by James B. Pritchard, American Journal of Archaeology, 72 (1968), pp. 391-393.

"Bethel Pottery of the Late Hellenistic and Early Roman Periods" in James L. Kelso, et al., "The Excavations of Bethel (1934-1960)," Annual of the American Schools of Oriental Research, 39 (1968), pp. 77-80.

"Bâb edh-Dhrâ', Perizzites and Emim," in Jerusalem through the Ages (Jerusalem: Israel Exploration Society, 1968), pp. 1-25.

1969

"Treatment of Cultural Property and Antiquities in Occupied Jordan," The Arab, 2 (Jan., 1969), pp. 6-7.

"Jordan" in E. Porada, ed., COWA Survey Western Asia (Area 15, No. 3, 1966; Boston: COWA, 1969), pp. 20-23.

"Jordan" in E. Porada, ed., <u>COWA Bibliography</u>: <u>Western Asia</u>
    (Area 15, No. 3, 1966; Boston: <u>COWA</u>, 1969), pp. 20-25.

"Tell Ta'annek," in <u>New Excavations 1968-69</u> (Jerusalem:
    Israel Department of Antiquities, 1969), pp. 41-42 (in
    Hebrew).

"A Ritual Incense Stand from Taanak," <u>Qadmoniot</u>, 2 (1969),
    pp. 16-17 (in Hebrew).

Review of FOUNDATION DEPOSITS IN ANCIENT MESOPOTAMIA, by
    Richard S. Ellis, <u>Journal of Biblical Literature</u>, 88
    (1969), pp. 494-496.

<u>Biblical Archaeology and History</u> (New York, 1969), ix + 129 pp.
    and 30 pls.

"The 1968 Excavations at Tell Ta'annek," <u>Bulletin of the American
    Schools of Oriental Research</u>, 195 (Oct., 1969), pp. 2-49.

"Tell Ta'annak" in "Chronique Archéologique," <u>Revue Biblique</u>,
    76 (1969), pp. 580-586.

Review of MODERN BIBLICAL STUDIES, edited by Dennis McCarthy
    and William Callen, <u>Perspective</u>, 10 (1969), pp. 262-263.

1970
    "Captive Treasures," <u>Mid East</u>, 10 (Feb., 1970), pp. 35-42.

"The Pottery of Palestine in the Persian Period," in <u>Archäolo-
    gie und Altes Testament</u>. Festschrift für Kurt Galling,
    ed. by A. Kuschke and E. Kutsch (Tübingen: J. C. B. Mohr,
    1970), pp. 179-197.

"'Captive Treasures,' Dr. Lapp replies," <u>Mid East</u>, 11 (Mar.,
    1970), p. 6.

"The Tell Deir 'Alla Challenge to Palestinian Archaeology,"
    review of EXCAVATIONS AT TELL DEIR 'ALLA I, by H. J.
    Franken, <u>Vestus Testamentum</u>, 20 (1970), pp. 243-256.

"Palestine in the Early Bronze Age," in <u>Near Eastern Archae-
    ology in the Twentieth Century</u>. Essays in honor of Nelson
    Glueck, ed. by J. A. Sanders (Garden City, N.Y.: Doubleday
    & Co., 1970), pp. 101-132.

Review of THE JUDGMENT OF THE DEAD: THE IDEA OF LIFE AFTER
DEATH IN THE MAJOR RELIGIONS, by S. G. F. Brandon,
Interpretation, 24 (1970), pp. 278-279.

"'Araq el-Emîr," in Encyclopaedia of Archaeological Excavations
in the Holy Land (Jerusalem: Israel Exploration Society
and Massada Ltd., 1970), pp. 467-469 (in Hebrew).

"Ta'anakh," in Encyclopaedia of Archaeological Excavations in
the Holy Land (Jerusalem: Israel Exploration Society and
Massada Ltd., 1970), pp. 626-628 (in Hebrew).

1971
Arabic for the Beginner in Archaeology. Revised and Enlarged
Edition (Bethlehem: Habash Press, 1971), 70 pp. (with
Najua Husseini, revision by Bishara Zoughbi).

Reprint of review of EXCAVATIONS AT TELL DEIR 'ALLA I by H. J.
Franken, Archeologia, 22 (1971), pp. 215-220.

1972
Review of NEW DIRECTIONS IN BIBLICAL ARCHAEOLOGY, ed. by D. N.
Freedman and J. C. Greenfield, Journal of Near Eastern
Studies, 31 (1972), p. 51.

NOTES

Chapter I

1. The investigations of Dr. Ute Lux since 1970 as a result of
the restoration of the Lutheran Church of the Redeemer in the
Muristan, Jerusalem, should be noted. Revue Biblique, 79 (1972),
pp. 577-578.

2. His death in September, 1971, cut short his still active life
of scholarship and field archaeology. It is a great loss to the
total international community.

3. See Chap. VI.

4. See Chap. VII.

5. See Chap. IX.

6. See Chap. XI.

7. See Chap. X.

8. See Chap. VIII.

9. See Chap. V.

10. See the recent discussions of "biblical archaeology" in the
Biblical Archaeologist, F. M. Cross, "W. F. Albright's View of
Biblical Archaeology and its Methodology," BA, 36 (1973), pp. 2-5,
and D. L. Holland, "Biblical Archaeology: an Onomastic Perplexity,"
BA, 37 (1974), pp. 19-23.

11. Attention may be drawn to the report by Roger Borass concerning the convergence of archaeology and the natural sciences in
research in the 1974-75 Newsletter, No. 2, of the American Schools
of Oriental Research. Though not very recent, cf. also, K. M.
Kenyon, Beginning in Archaeology (New York: Praeger, 1957),
Appendixes II-V.

12. The author, P. W. Lapp, considered these first three chapters
as introductory to an updating of the finds of Palestinian archaeology. See the Introduction.

13. For a fuller discussion of the relationship of archaeology,
history, and biblical studies see P. W. Lapp, Biblical Archaeology
and History (Cleveland: World Publishers, 1969).

Chapter II

1.   A recent practice in Israel has been for colleges to offer academic credit to student volunteers for "tuition courses". Financial aid as well as labor is supplied by those who wish to participate. Volunteer programs include those at Gezer, Tell el-Hesi, Khirbet Shema', Caesarea, and Tell Dan.

2.   See Chap. IX, pp. 92-93, for plans by the Taanach expedition.

3.   This especially applies to student volunteers. See n. 1 above.

4.   The following discussion excludes "volunteers" who do the work of laborers on digs.

5.   The last five years have seen advancement in what is often described as the "new" archaeology. See, for example, L. E. Toombs, "Tell el-Hesi, 1970-71," Palestine Exploration Quarterly, 1974, pp. 19-23; L. E. Stager, et al., ed., American Expedition to Idalion, Cyprus (First Preliminary Report: Seasons of 1971 and 1972, Cambridge, Mass.: American Schools of Oriental Research, 1974), especially, p. 1. Attention may also be drawn to a recent book presenting a new method of typology in ceramic studies whereby the pottery is analysed on the production processes. H. J. Franken, In Search of the Jericho Potters, Amsterdam and New York: North-Holland Publishing Co., 1974. Franken first presented these methods in Vol. I of his Deir 'Allā excavations (Chap. III, n. 7), which P. W. Lapp thought had great potentialities. See his review, "The Tell Deir 'Allā Challenge to Palestinian Archaeology," Vetus Testamentum, 20 (1970), pp. 243-256.

6.   W. F. Albright, The Archaeology of Palestine and the Bible (New York: Revel, 1932), p. 26.

7.   The latest edition is: J. D. Seger, Handbook for Field Operations (New York: Hebrew Union College, 1971).

Chapter III

1.   W. F. Albright, "The Excavation of Tell Beit Mirsim," Vols. I, IA, II, III, Annual of the American Schools of Oriental Research, XII, XIII, XVII, XXI-XXII (New Haven: American Schools of Oriental Research, 1932-1943).

2.   G. E. Wright, The Pottery of Palestine from the Earliest Times to the End of the Early Bronze Age (New Haven: ASOR, 1957).

3.   P. W. Lapp, Palestinian Ceramic Chronology, 200 B.C. - A.D. 70 (New Haven: ASOR, 1961). Henceforth PCC.

4.   F. Zayadine, "Early Hellenistic Pottery," Annual of the Department of Antiquities of Jordan, XI (1966), pp. 53-64; N. Lapp, "Pottery from Some Hellenistic Loci at Balâtah (Shechem)," Bulletin of the American Schools of Oriental Research, 175 (1964), pp. 14-26.

5.   P. W. Lapp, "The Pottery of Palestine in the Persian Period," in Archäologie und Altes Testament, Festschrift für Kurt Galling, ed. A. Kuschke and E. Kutsch (Tübingen: J. C. B. Mohr, 1970), pp. 179-197.

6.   See now, especially the Heshbon studies of J. Sauer, Heshbon Pottery 1971 (Berrien Springs, Michigan: Andrews University Press, 1973).

7.   J. B. Hennessy, The Foreign Relations of Palestine during the Early Bronze Age (London: Bernard Quaritch Ltd., 1967); K. M. Kenyon, Excavations at Jericho, Vols. I, II (London: British School of Archaeology in Jerusalem, 1960, 1965); J. W. Crowfoot, G. M. Crowfoot, and K. M. Kenyon, The Objects from Samaria (Samaria-Sebaste, III [London: Palestine Exploration Fund, 1957]); H. K. Franken, Excavations at Tell Deir 'Allā, Vol. I (Leiden: E. J. Brill, 1969).

8.   For more recent studies concerning scientific methods of dating, including the new half life and Suess bristlecone pine calibration, see The Impact of the Natural Sciences on Archaeology (A Joint Symposium of the Royal Society and the British Academy [London: The British Academy and Oxford University Press, 1970]).

9.   See Chap. XI, pp. 111-112, for the description of the daily schedule at the 1967 Tell er-Rumeith excavation.

10.   The manuscript was completed to this point in 1970. The following section is the work of the editor, Nancy L. Lapp, in 1974.

11.   G. E. Wright, "The Archaeology of Palestine," in The Bible and the Ancient Near East, ed. G. E. Wright (Garden City, N.Y.: Doubleday & Co., 1961). Henceforth BANE.

12.   R. de Vaux, O.P., Palestine During the Neolithic and Chalcolithic Periods and Palestine in the Early Bronze Age (Cambridge Ancient History, revised ed., Fasc. 47 and 46, 1966 [Vol. I, Chap. IX(b) and Chap. XVI], Cambridge: Cambridge University Press, 1966).

138

Notes to Page 46

13. G. E. Wright, "The Archaeology of Palestine from the Neolithic through the Middle Bronze Age," Journal of the American Oriental Society, XCI (1971), pp. 276-293. The most important excavations for this period have undoubtedly been K. Kenyon's at Jericho (Digging Up Jericho, Archaeology in the Holy Land [New York: Praeger, 1957, 1970], Jericho I and II [see n. 7 above]), but the final report on the tell has not yet appeared. These excavations must be supplemented by the continuing work of J. Kaplan, J. Perrot, and H. de Contenson (for bibliography see de Vaux, n. 12 above, and Wright, n. 13 above, as well as recent reports in the Revue Biblique and Israel Exploration Journal).

14. Wright, JAOS, XCI, p. 277, notes that Jericho Pre-pottery Neolithic B is related to the Tahunian culture, following de Vaux. Then, after a gap, Jericho IX (= Kenyon's Pottery Neolithic A) falls within the pottery Neolithic, whereas Jericho VIII (= Kenyon's Pottery Neolithic B) can be considered Early Chalcolithic along with the Yamukian and J. Kaplan's Wadi Rabah cultures (pp. 278-279).

15. P. W. Lapp, "Palestine in the Early Bronze Age," Near Eastern Archaeology in the Twentieth Century, Essays in Honor of Nelson Glueck, ed. J. A. Sanders (Garden City, N.Y.: Doubleday & Co., 1970), pp. 101-131. R. T. Schaub, "The Early Bronze IA - IB Pottery of the Bâb edh-Dhrâ' Cemetery, Jordan," Ph.D. dissertation, University of Pittsburgh, 1973, pp. 294-297, and "An Early Bronze IV Tomb from Bâb edh-Dhrâ'," Bulletin of the American Schools of Oriental Research, 210 (1973), pp. 17-18.

16. W. G. Dever, "The EB IV-MB I Horizon in Transjordan and Southern Palestine," BASOR, 210 (1973), pp. 37-63. Note especially the chart on p. 38, and p. 41, n. 8.

17. Wright, JAOS, XCI, pp. 289-291.

18. See, for example, R. Amiran, Ancient Pottery of the Holy Land (Jerusalem: Masada Press, 1969), p. 124.

19. Amiran, p. 191.

20. Note, for example, the seventh and sixth century strata at Beth-zur (The 1957 Excavation at Beth-zur, Annual of the American Schools of Oriental Research, XXXVIII, pp. 26-29); Tell Beit Mirsim (AASOR, XXI-XXII, p. 145); Hesbon (E. Lugenbeal and J. Sauer, "Seventh-Sixth Century B.C. Pottery from Area B at Heshbon," Andrews University Seminary Studies, X [1972], pp. 62-64); and Tell el-Fûl (forthcoming AASOR volume and see Chap. VIII below).

21. For example, Wright, n. 11 above, and Amiran, n. 18 above.

22. See n. 5 above.

23. This will be amplified in the forthcoming publication of
the 1964 Tell el-Fûl excavation where Stratum III B dated within
this period. Note P. W. Lapp's designation "Babylonian" for this
period in PCC (n. 3 above), p. 4. Wright calls this period Iron
II C (BANE, p. 96), which has some advantages, but I have chosen
to stay away from this designation not only because of its use for
the period 800-587 B.C. in some publications (Amiran, p. 191), but
also because archaeological evidence supports changes in Palestine
at this time.

24. Galling (n. 5 above), p. 185.

25. PCC, p. 4, n. 20.

26. Sauer, Heshbon Pottery 1971, pp. 1-5.

Chapter IV

1. Reprinted from The Biblical Archaeologist, XXVI (Dec., 1963),
pp. 121-134, with slight editorial changes. Used by permission.
Although this article was written in 1963 and a large amount of
excavation has taken place in Palestine in the past twelve years,
the situation has not substantially changed. This was predicted
p. 55 below. Note, however, two reports of recent years which
summarize the vast amount of archaeology going on: American
School of Oriental Research Newsletter, 1972-73, #1, "Archaeology
in Israel: An Embarrassment of Riches," and Newsletter, 1973-74,
#9, the annual report of the late president of the American Schools,
G. E. Wright.

2. Nelson Glueck, "Explorations in Eastern Palestine, IV," Annual
of the American Schools of Oriental Research, XXV-XXVIII, Part I
(1951), pp. xviii-xix. Only about three quarters of the sites in
North Gilead were included and some sites near the mouth of the
Yarmuk had not been examined. To these some sites in an area between Amman and the Jordan River as well as a few not easily access-
ible on the east bank of the Dead Sea may now be added.

3. Nelson Glueck, Rivers in the Desert (1959), p. x.

4. See Chap. VII.

5. See Chap. VI.

6.   Ivar Lissner, "The Tomb of Moses Is Still Undiscovered,"
Biblical Archaeologist, XXVI.3 (1963), pp. 106-108.

7.   See Chap. IX.

8.   See Chap. VI.

9.   See Chap. V.

10.   See Chap. XI.

11.   See Chap. VIII.

12.   L. E. Toombs and G. E. Wright, Bulletin of the American
School of Oriental Research, No. 169 (Feb. 1963), esp. pp. 17-18;
cf. Wright, Illustrated London News, Aug. 10, 1963, pp. 204-208.

13.   See Chap. VII.

Chapter V

1.   The bulk of this chapter, particularly that concerning the
third campaign, is contained in an article written April 10, 1964,
at the American School of Oriental Research, Jerusalem, Jordan,
for the Annual of the Department of Antiquities of Jordan, X
(1965), pp. 37-42.

2.   This brief discussion is based largely on her detailed
discussion of the fountain in Bulletin of the American Schools
of Oriental Research, 171 (Oct., 1963), pp. 44-55.

3.   See Annual of the Department of Antiquities of Jordan, Vols.
VI-VII (1962), p. 83.

4.   Bulletin of the American Schools of Oriental Research, 171
(Oct., 1963), pp. 39-45.

5.   Syria, Vol. 27 (1950), pp. 82-136.

6.   For location see Pl. 2; cf. ADAJ, VI-VII, pp. 85-87.

7.   Antiq. XII, 233.

Chapter VI

1.   Archaeological Newsletter of the American Schools of Oriental Research, 1962-1963, #8. Used with permission.

2.   Archaeological Newsletter of the American Schools of Oriental Research, 1963-1964, #4. Used with permission.

3.   See Chap. VII.

Chapter VII

1.   Extracted from the Archaeological Newsletter, American Schools of Oriental Research, 1963-1964, #1. Used with permission.

2.   K. M. Kenyon, Excavations at Jericho, I (London: British School of Archaeology in Jerusalem, 1960), p. 183; Revue Biblique, 67 (1960), p. 602.

3.   See the further discussion of these problems concerning the identity of these people and their relation to the Biblical patriarchs in Chapter VIII of the final publication. P. W. Lapp, The Dhahr Mirzbâneh Tombs, New Haven, 1966, pp. 86-116.

Chapter VIII

1.   The basis of this chapter is the Archaeological Newsletter, American Schools of Oriental Research, 1963-1964, #6, with some changes and additions based upon further research and the article, "Tell el-Fûl," The Biblical Archaeologist, XXVIII (Feb., 1965), pp. 2-10. Used by permission.

2.   See Annual of the American Schools of Oriental Research, IV (1922-23), and XXXIV-XXXV (1954-56).

3.   Lawrence A. Sinclair, "An Archaeological Study of Gibeah," Biblical Archaeologist, XXVII, No. 2 (May, 1964), Fig. 14.

4.   See P. W. Lapp, "The Pottery of Palestine in the Persian Period," in Archäologie und Altes Testament, Festschrift für Kurt Galling, A. Kuschke and E. Kutsch, eds., (Tübingen, 1970), pp. 179-197, esp. n. 14.

Notes to Pages 91-98

Chapter IX

1. Reprinted in part from The Biblical Archaeologist, XXX (Feb., 1967), pp. 2-27.

2. These texts refer to "Taanach and its towns". It seems preferable for modern usage to consider Taanach a town and translate "Taanach and its villages".

3. Tell Ta'annek (Vienna, 1904) and Eine Nachlese auf dem Tell Ta'annek in Palästina (Vienna, 1905).

4. See Postscript to this chapter.

5. W. F. Albright, BASOR, 94 (April, 1944), p. 27, and A. Malamat, Scripta Hierosolymitana, VIII (1961), 219. The arguments are not compelling, and it is not inconceivable that the tablets were written before 1468 B.C. or may even have been related to the campaign of Tuthmosis III.

6. See the evidence for the slight extension of the LB occupation into the fourteenth century and the further discussion of the early occupation after the third campaign, BASOR, 195 (Oct., 1969), pp. 4-5.

7. Albright, The Archaeology of Palestine (London, 1960), p. 117.

8. Ibid.

9. This section is summarized from pp. 10-22 of "Taanach by the Waters of Megiddo," BA, XXX.

10. D. R. Hillers, "An Alphabetic Cuneiform Tablet from Taanach (TT 433)," BASOR, 173 (1964), pp. 45-50.

11. For another translation see F. M. Cross, "The Canaanite Cuneiform Tablet from Ta'anach," BASOR, 190 (1968), pp. 41-46.

12. P. L. O. Guy, Megiddo Tombs (Chicago, 1938), p. 177 and Pl. 115:11, 24.

13. R. Young, American Journal of Archaeology, LXVI (1962), 154.

14. R. de Vaux, Revue Biblique, LXIV (1957), 559-567. Cf. also his article in the Eissfeldt Festschrift Von Ugarit nach Qumran (Berlin, 1958), pp. 250-265.

15. *Megiddo II*, pp. 44-45, Figs. 100-102, and Pl. 285, from Stratum V A.

16. E.g., *BASOR*, 173, p. 40 under Fig. 21.

17. For references see *BASOR*, 173, p. 39, n. 62.

18. G. M Crowfoot, *Palestine Exploration Quarterly*, (1940), pp. 150-153.

19. See footnote 15 above.

20. G. Schumacher, *Tell el-Mutsellim*, I (Leipzig, 1908), pp. 105-110.

21. Cf. *BASOR*, 173, p. 28 with n. 41.

22. *Megiddo Tombs*, esp. Pls. 128-130.

23. For details, see *BASOR*, 173, pp. 39-41.

24. The following is summarized from reports of the third campaign in 1968 in order to include the results of the last season of excavation. For fuller accounts see *Revue Biblique*, 76 (1969), pp. 580-586, and *BASOR*, 195 (1969), pp. 2-49.

Chapter X

1. From Archaeological Newsletter, 1964-65, #5, of the American Schools of Oriental Research. Used with permission.

2. "Early Bronze Pottery from Bâb ed-Drâ in Moab," *Bulletin of the American Schools of Oriental Research*, 95 (Oct., 1944), pp. 3-11.

3. *Ibid.*, p. 5, Pl. 1, esp. Nos. 43, 45, 47-49.

4. Reprinted with permission from "Bâb edh-Dhrâ', Perizzites and Emin," *Jerusalem Through the Ages*, Jerusalem, The Israel Exploration Society, 1968, pp. 5-10.

5. For the dating and detailed description of the earliest tombs see my article in the *Bulletin of the American Schools of Oriental Research*, 189 (1968), pp. 12-41.

6. See ref. in n. 6.

7. The most recent summary is J. B. Hennessy, <u>The Foreign
Relations of Palestine during the Early Bronze Age</u> (London,
1967). The dates here proposed are lower because I follow a
lower Egyptian chronology.

Chapter XI

1. From American Schools of Oriental Research, Newsletter,
#6, 1967-1968. Used with permission.

2. The substance of this enterprise was translated from a
Newsletter to the <u>Revue Biblique</u>, 70 (1963), pp. 406-411.

3. Gustavus F. Swift, Jr., "The Pottery of the 'Amuq Phases
K to O, and its Historical Relationships" (unpublished Ph.D.
dissertation, Department of Oriental Languages and Civilizations,
University of Chicago, 1958).

4. <u>Israel Exploration Journal</u>, 14 (1964), p. 32, n. 99.